The Crisis
Cookbook

The Crisis Cookbook

Edited by Nicholas Lander

MARKS &
SPENCER

Marks and Spencer p.l.c.
PO Box 3339
Chester CH99 9QS

shop online
www.marksandspencer.com

ISBN 978-1-899257-56-0
Typeset by Palimpsest Book Production Limited
Printed in Great Britain by Clays Ltd

INTRODUCTION

For the past 18 years I have had the good fortune to be the restaurant correspondent of the Financial Times which has brought me into close contact, and invariably close friendship, with some of the best chefs in the world. Their expertise and generosity with their recipes form the basis of this book.

I have also been involved for a shorter period of time with the remarkable Crisis at Christmas event when volunteers for this charity for homeless people look after, feed and revive many of London's homeless during the week between Christmas and New Year. This has seen me cooking over 200 fried eggs one cold December morning; unpacking and washing a huge amount of kitchen equipment; and one day, before the cooking started, sharpening about 400 knives so the volunteer chefs could begin to do their jobs properly.

On December 23rd 2006 I was in a Crisis kitchen in the City looking out of the window as the queue of those waiting to come into the warmth of their temporary shelter was growing and I began to ask myself how I could put my professional contacts to good use, to provide Crisis with additional funds to do their job even more efficiently. This cookbook is the result.

Above all this book is meant to be fun and inspirational. It is obviously very 'cheffy' in that all the contributors are professional chefs so it is not intended for the absolute beginner. Some of the recipes are much easier than others and anyone who wants to have a go at Ferran Adrià's first or main course recipe is undoubtedly setting themselves quite a challenge (his dessert by contrast is very straightforward).

But there are many much easier recipes and for me one of the attractions is the opportunity to create from one slim volume a dinner party where the first course is inspired by Paul Bocuse, the main course comes from Simon Hopkinson and the dessert is one of three supplied by Clare Clark, the lovely English pastry chef now based at The French Laundry in California. And because they are all

1

such talented chefs I have not dared to supply an editorial voice — as you see them is as they cook from them.

The only condition I laid down for the 28 chefs is that their recipes are not particularly associated with Christmas — they are to be enjoyed at any time of the year. This is not only to make the book far more useful but also to reflect the fact that although Crisis may best be known for its well-publicised work for homeless people at Christmas its challenge of helping the homeless goes on all year long.

The chefs have kindly donated all these recipes without charge so my biggest thanks must go to them and to my wife, Jancis Robinson, for her articles on wine which follow the recipes. Julia Harding MW, Sam Hart and Marie-Pierre Moine have been kind enough to help with translations and Lynne Simmonds has provided some delightful illustrations. Silvija Davidson came to my rescue and read through all the recipes to enable them to be cooked from at home for which I am most grateful.

My biggest thanks, however, must go to Samantha Borland, Andrew Henty, Esther Hollingworth, Julia Connolly and Lisa Simmonds at Penguin who patiently listened to my idea for this book and then professionally turned it into reality. Without them this book would simply not have happened.

Finally, the cost of printing this book has been entirely underwritten by supporters of Crisis to ensure that it generates as much money as possible for this very worthwhile organisation. Thanks to Stora Enso, Clays and Palimpsest for their generous contributions towards the paper, printing and typesetting costs of these books.

Nick Lander.

CONTENTS

Ferran Adrià, El Bulli, Spain, 5

Mario Batali, Babbo, New York, 11

Vineet Bhatia, Rasoi Vineet Bhatia, London, 17

Heston Blumenthal, The Fat Duck, Bray, 27

Paul Bocuse, Collonges-au-Mont-d'Or, France, 41

Clare Clark, pastry chef, The French Laundry, California, 47

Sam and Sam Clark, Moro, London, 53

Sally Clarke, Clarke's, London, 61

Anthony Demetre, Arbutus, London, 69

Alain Ducasse, Le Louis XV, Monaco, 73

James and Emma Faulks, Magdalen, London, 79

Chris Galvin, Galvin's, London, 87

Fergus Henderson, St John, London, 93

Henry Harris, Racine, London, 99

Shaun Hill, The Glasshouse, Worcester, 107

Baba Hine, The Corse Lawn Hotel, 117

Mark Hix, Chef/Director, Caprice Restaurants, London, 123

Ken Hom, 133

Simon Hopkinson, 139

Nigel Howarth, Northcote Manor, Lancashire, 145

Tom Kitchin, Kitchin's, Leith, Scotland, 155

Jeremy Lee, The Blueprint Café, London, 161

Rowley Leigh, Le Café Anglais, London,   167

Bruce Poole, Chez Bruce, London,   175

Joël Robuchon, L'Atelier du Robuchon,   183

Michael Romano, Union Square Café, New York,   189

Rick Stein, The Seafood Restaurant, Padstow,   197

Alice Waters, Chez Panisse, California.   205

Ferran Adrià

21st Century Tortilla
Langoustines with Ceps 1992
Apricots with ice cream

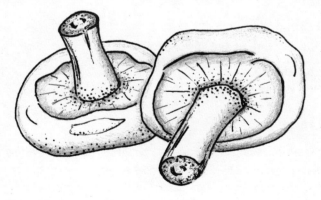

21ST CENTURY TORTILLA

SERVES 4

FOR THE WARM POTATO FOAM:
250g mashing potatoes
100ml cooking water from the potatoes
125ml whipping cream
35ml virgin olive oil
2 iSi 0.5 litre soda siphons charged with N_2O

FOR THE ONION CONFIT:
250g onions
90g virgin olive oil of 0.4% (very low) acidity
100ml water
salt

FOR THE EGG SABAYON:
40g egg yolks
30ml boiling water
salt

FOR THE YOLK SAUCE:
40g pasteurised egg yolk

TO FINISH:
50g virgin olive oil

METHOD

1. Peel and chop the potatoes then boil in salted water, starting from cold, for approximately 20 minutes. When they have finished cooking, drain, reserving the cooking water. Put the potato and 100ml of the cooking water in a thermomix set at 60°C. Blend, adding the cream little by little. Do the same with the oil until you have a fine homogenous emulsion. Season carefully with salt. Sieve and fill the siphons using a funnel. Charge the siphons and place in a bain-marie at 70°C.

2. Peel the onion, chop in four then slice into fine juliennes. Gently fry the onion in the olive oil, stirring continuously. It should take on a beautiful golden colour. Drain off the excess oil and deglaze the pan with a little water. Cook until evaporated. Repeat the procedure until the mixture takes on the texture and colour of caramelised jam. Season carefully with salt and set aside.

3. Place the yolks in a bowl, beat with a hand whisk and add the boiling water in a thin stream, whisking all the time. Beat vigorously over a moderate heat until the sabayon emulsifies. Season carefully with salt.

4. Pass yolks for the sauce though a sieve and keep in a sauce bottle.

FINISHING AND PRESENTATION

In a martini glass place in this order:

1. A tablespoon of the onion confit, heated until very hot.

2. A tablespoon of the egg yolk sauce.

3. Two tablespoons of the sabayon.

4. Check that the siphons containing the potatoes are hot. Shake energetically, then fill the glass stopping 1cm from the top. Finish with a drizzle of virgin olive oil.

FERRAN ADRIÀ

7

LANGOUSTINES WITH CEPS 1992

SERVES 4

FOR THE LANGOUSTINES:
4 langoustines weighing 90g each

FOR THE YOUNG GARLIC:
12 cloves young garlic

FOR THE INVOLTINI OF CEPS AND LANGOUSTINES:
2 ceps measuring 8cm across the top
4 langoustine tails (see Method)
salt
virgin olive oil of 0.4% (very low) acidity

FOR THE CEP OIL:
50g cep trimmings (see Method)
100ml sunflower oil
½ garlic clove
½ bay leaf

FOR THE PINE NUT VINAIGRETTE:
40g toasted pine nuts
40g cep oil (see above)
5g finely chopped chives
sherry vinegar
salt

TO FINISH:
virgin olive oil of 0.4% (very low) acidity
salt
8 sprigs fresh chervil

METHOD

1. Decapitate the langoustines and shell the tails.
2. Very carefully remove the intestines from each tail.

3. Cut 20 dead man's fingers into 0.6cm lengths.
4. Blanch the garlic cloves for 30 seconds in hot water.
5. Remove the outer layer and the inside root from each of the garlic cloves.
6. For the cep involtini, separate the caps from the stalks.
7. Clean the caps with a damp cloth.
8. Slice the caps horizontally into 0.2cm-thin slices.
9. Keep the trimmings from the ceps.
10. Arrange the sliced ceps to form 4 involtini 'wrappers', each of them the same length as the langoustine tails.
11. Lightly cook in a hot pan with a little olive oil so that each involtino just softens a little without taking on any colour.
12. Carefully salt the ceps and langoustines.
13. Wrap each langoustine in a cep involtino.
14. Confit the cep trimmings in the sunflower oil at 70°C for 1 hour.
15. Remove from the heat, do not drain, refrigerate for 24 hours.
16. Chop half the pine nuts as finely as possible to obtain a powder.
17. Roughly chop the other half to form bigger pieces.
18. In a bowl mix together both types of chopped pinenuts with the cep oil.
19. Add the chives and season with salt and the sherry vinegar.

FINISHING AND PRESENTATION

1. In a hot pan sear the tender garlic cloves and then peel off the outer layer.
2. Heat some olive oil in another pan.
3. Cook the cep-wrapped langoustines.
4. Arrange 3 garlic cloves on each of four round plates then scatter 5 dead man's fingers on each plate.
5. Place a langoustine involtino in the middle of each plate without breaking any of the dead man's fingers.

APRICOTS WITH ICE CREAM

SERVES 8

4 apricots
4 strands of saffron
1 vanilla pod, split
1 lemon grass stalk
1 tbsp honey

½ litre vanilla ice cream

METHOD

1. Remove the stones from the apricots.

2. Place the apricots on silver foil and scatter with the saffron, seeds from the vanilla pod, the lemon grass sliced into thin rounds and the honey.

3. Seal the foil like an envelope and cook under the grill or in the oven.

4. Plate the apricots and garnish with a little of the cooking juices and the ice cream.

Mario Batali

Peperonata con Bruschetta
Penne con Cavolofiore
Beef Braciole

PEPERONATA CON BRUSCHETTA

This simple bruschetta captures the heart of September in Puglia when the deep-coloured peppers are at their sweetest and everything in the garden is singing. On a hot day this makes a great lunch with a bitter salad and a glass of raisiny Ciro.

SERVES 6

4 tbsp, plus 3 tbsp extra virgin olive oil
1 red onion cut into 5mm dice
2 sweet red bell peppers, cored, seeded and cut into 10mm dice
2 sweet yellow peppers, cored, seeded and cut into 10mm dice
2 tbsp Sherry vinegar
2 tbsp fresh marjoram leaves
salt and pepper
6 x 2.5cm thick slices country bread

METHOD

1. In a 30–35 cm sauté pan, heat 4 tablespoons olive oil over high heat until almost smoking.

2. Add the onion and the peppers and sauté over high heat for 4 minutes, until browned at the edges and softened.

3. Add the Sherry vinegar and salt and pepper to taste, reduce the heat to medium, and continue to cook for 5 to 7 minutes, until the peppers are tender. Adjust seasoning and set aside to cool. Add marjoram and stir through.

4. Preheat the grill or broiler. Grill each slice of bread on both sides until crusty and browned, then top with peperonata. Drizzle with remaining oil and serve.

PENNE CON CAVOLOFIORE

They say in the States that cruciferous vegetables are the colon's little broom. Well, housekeeping never tasted so good!!!

SERVES 6

120ml extra virgin olive oil
1 clove garlic, peeled and crushed
1 tbsp capers, rinsed and drained
1 tsp chilli flakes
1kg tomatoes, peeled, seeded and chopped, or 2 cups canned whole tomatoes, drained and chopped
1 cauliflower head, trimmed and broken into 2.5cm florets
salt and pepper
500g dry penne
2 bunches Italian parsley, finely chopped to yield ½ cup
50g freshly grated Parmigiano Reggiano or pecorino cheese

METHOD

1. In a 30–35 cm sauté pan, heat the olive oil over medium heat and add the garlic. Cook gently until softened and very light golden brown, then add the capers, the chilli flakes and the tomatoes and cook, stirring, until the tomatoes begin to break down.

2. Add the cauliflower florets and stir well. Add half a cup (about 120ml) very hot water, lower heat to medium and cook for 30 minutes, or until the cauliflower is very tender.

3. Bring 6 litres of water to a boil and add 2 tablespoons salt. Add the penne and cook according to package directions, until tender yet al dente. Drain and add to the pan containing the cauliflower.

4. Stir in parsley and black pepper to taste and toss for a minute over high heat. Divide evenly among 6 warmed pasta bowls, top with grated cheese and serve immediately.

BEEF BRACIOLE

These tasty little packets are great braised like this for the cooler months, but are also excellent cooked on the grill in the summer, served simply with sliced tomatoes and onions, and dressed in good oil with lots of freshly cracked black pepper.

SERVES 4

8 thin boneless beef cutlets, from shoulder or flank, pounded thin
8 thin slices pancetta, plus 2 tablespoons finely chopped pancetta
3 cloves garlic, finely chopped, plus 1 clove, coarsely chopped
1 bunch Italian parsley, finely chopped to yield ¼ cup
3 tbsp capers, rinsed and drained
50g pecorino cheese, grated, plus a further 50g
2 oranges, zest and juice
4 tbsp extra-virgin olive oil
1 onion, coarsely chopped
1 carrot, finely chopped
120ml dry red wine
500ml canned tomatoes, coarsely chopped, with juices
¼ tsp chilli flakes
salt and pepper

METHOD

1. Lay each beef cutlet over a slice of pancetta, then sprinkle each with a little finely chopped garlic and some finely chopped parsley.

2. Add a few capers, a teaspoon of the grated pecorino and a bit of orange zest to each cutlet. Roll each up and secure with a toothpick or tie with thread.

3. Heat a deep skillet over medium-high heat, add the olive oil and

brown the beef rolls 4 at a time on all sides, about 6 minutes. Remove as they brown and set aside.

4. Add the chopped pancetta to the pan, along with the onion, coarsely chopped garlic and carrot, lower the heat to medium-low and cook, stirring occasionally, until the vegetables are soft but not brown.

5. Add the orange juice and wine, increase the heat slightly and cook, scraping any brown bits. When the liquid is reduced by half, add the tomatoes and continue cooking for 5 minutes, to reduce and thicken into a sauce.

6. Stir the chilli flakes into the pan and add the beef rolls, spooning sauce over to cover well. Season with salt and pepper and reduce the heat to medium-low.

7. Cover the pan and cook 25 minutes. Allow to rest 5 minutes, then place the rolls on a plate, spoon sauce over and serve with extra grated cheese on the side.

Vineet Bhatia

Almond Crusted Potato Tikki . . .
Oven Roasted Broccoli . . .
Grilled Paneer, Saffron . . .
Roasted Fruit Kebab
Chocolate Rabdi

ALMOND CRUSTED POTATO TIKKI, GRILLED ASPARAGUS, GREEN HERB CHUTNEY

SERVES 4

FOR THE ALMOND TIKKI:
300g potatoes, peeled, boiled and coarsely mashed
30ml vegetable oil
1 tsp cumin seeds
¾ tsp chopped green chilli
1 tsp chopped fresh ginger
2 tbsp chopped red onion
1 tbsp chopped fresh coriander
salt
vegetable oil for deep frying

FOR THE BATTER:
100g plain flour
1 tsp red chilli powder
½ tsp turmeric powder
salt
cold water to form a thick batter

FOR THE GRILLED ASPARAGUS:
1 tbsp ghee
20 Thai baby asparagus, blanched
½ tsp black peppercorns, crushed
salt

FOR THE GREEN HERB CHUTNEY:
50g fresh coriander, roughly chopped
25g fresh mint, roughly chopped
30g Greek yoghurt
1 tsp chopped garlic
1 tsp chopped fresh ginger
1 tsp chopped green chilli

½ tsp sugar
salt

METHOD

Almond Tikki:

1. Heat the oil in a pan to medium heat and add the cumin seeds. As they splutter add the green chilli, ginger and onion. Sauté for a minute, stirring.

2. At this stage, add the potatoes and salt and blend the mixture with the back of the spoon.

3. Turn the mixture out into a flat tray to cool and finally add the coriander.

4. Shape the potato mixture into 4cm flat discs.

5. Dip into the batter (see below), remove all excess batter and place into a dish of flaked almonds. Turn to coat.

6. Deep fry in medium hot oil till the almonds turn golden.

Batter:

1. Put all the ingredients into a steel bowl, add cold water and mix well to form a smooth thick batter.

Grilled Asparagus:

1. Pour the ghee onto a hot griddle, arrange the asparagus on the griddle and cook for a minute, turning at least once. Remove and season with salt and pepper.

Green Herb Chutney:

1. Put all the ingredients into a blender and blend to a smooth paste.

OVEN ROASTED BROCCOLI, RED ONION AND CUMIN KHICHDI

SERVES 4

FOR THE BROCCOLI:
1 medium size crown of broccoli, cut into florets
1 tsp chopped green chilli
1 tsp chopped fresh ginger
1 tbsp chopped fresh coriander
2 tbsp Greek yoghurt
50ml single cream
50g Cheddar cheese, grated
½ tsp finely ground black pepper
salt

METHOD

1. Blanch the broccoli florets in salted hot water, drain and run under cold water to prevent further cooking. Drain and set aside.

2. Place all the remaining ingredients in a steel bowl and mix well to form a paste.

3. Place the blanched broccoli florets into the marinade and set aside for at least 2 hours to absorb the flavours.

4. Place the broccoli in a roasting tray and roast in a preheated oven set to 190°C/Gas mark 5 for 4 minutes.

FOR THE RED ONION AND CUMIN KHICHDI:
3 tbsp vegetable oil
1 tsp cumin seeds
1 tbsp chopped garlic
1 medium size red onion, chopped
1 tbsp chopped fresh ginger

1 tbsp chopped green chilli
1 tsp turmeric powder
150g Basmati rice
450ml vegetable stock
3 tbsp Greek yoghurt, whipped
1 tbsp butter
salt
1 tbsp chopped fresh coriander

METHOD

1. Heat the oil in a pan to medium heat, add cumin seeds, and as they begin to splutter add the chopped garlic.

2. Sauté for a minute and add the chopped onion, ginger and green chilli. Sauté for 2 minutes.

3. Add the turmeric powder and the rice and cook for a further 2 minutes.

4. Now pour in the warmed vegetable stock, bring the mixture to a boil, reduce heat and simmer until the rice is three-quarters done, and the stock absorbed.

5. Add the whipped yoghurt and salt and continue cooking until the rice is done.

6. Lastly, add the butter and chopped coriander, and stir in.

7. Serve with the broccoli.

GRILLED PANEER, SAFFRON AND GREEN PEA UPMA WITH CHILLI OIL AND CRISP CURRY LEAVES

SERVES 4

FOR THE GRILLED PANEER:
300g paneer, cut into triangles

FOR THE MARINADE:
1 tsp ginger paste
1 tsp garlic paste
3 tbsp Greek yoghurt
1 tsp lemon juice
1 tsp Kashmiri red chilli powder
½ tsp turmeric powder
½ tsp cumin powder
½ tsp coriander powder
½ tsp garam masala powder
½ tsp cardamom seeds
salt

FOR THE SAFFRON UPMA:
3 tbsp ghee
1 tbsp mustard seeds
1 tsp chopped fresh ginger
1 tsp chopped green chilli
2 tbsp finely chopped shallots
6 curry leaves, coarsely chopped
6 tbsp fine semolina
1 tbsp saffron water
100g green peas, blanched
225ml water, warmed
salt

METHOD

Paneer:

1. In a steel bowl mix together all the marinade ingredients.

2. Place the paneer triangles in the marinade and stir well.

3. Skewer onto bamboo sticks and cook under the grill or in a hot oven until the paneer softens and takes on a golden colour.

Saffron Upma:

1. In a pan, heat the ghee and add the mustard seeds. As they begin to pop and release their aromas, add the ginger, green chilli and shallots.

2. Sauté the mixture for 2 minutes then add the curry leaves, sauté for a further minute, then add the semolina.

3. Reduce the heat and fry the semolina until its nutty aromas are released, this should take approximately 4–5 minutes.

4. At this stage, add the saffron water and green peas. Blend the peas into the semolina and pour in the warm water, stirring all the time to prevent any lumps forming.

5. Lastly, add the salt and mix it well into the upma. The resulting mixture should have the consistency of mash.

ROASTED FRUIT KEBAB WITH SWEET SPICES, WHITE CHOCOLATE RABDI AND SAFFRON ICE CREAM

SERVES 4

FOR THE ROASTED FRUIT KEBAB:
8 bamboo skewers, 12.5cm length
8 x 2.5cm cubes golden pineapple
4 strawberries, halved
1 apple, peeled and cut into 2.5cm cubes
2 kiwi fruit, peeled and quartered

FOR THE SPICED BUTTER:
100g unsalted butter, softened
60g brown Demerara sugar
1 tsp orange zest
2 tbsp orange juice
½ tsp green cardamom powder
½ tsp cinnamon powder
½ tsp fennel seed powder

FOR THE WHITE CHOCOLATE RABDI:
100ml double cream
40g white chocolate

METHOD

Fruit Skewers:

1. Skewer a piece of each fruit on a skewer (2 skewers per portion).

2. In a steel bowl mix together all the ingredients for the spiced butter and blend well.

3. Rub the butter over the skewered fruit and set aside for 30 minutes.

4. Place the skewers on a roasting tray and cook in a moderately hot oven for 5 minutes. Serve with saffron ice cream and chocolate rabdi (see below).

Chocolate Rabdi:

1. Bring the cream to a boil and simmer till it thickens slightly.

2. Remove from the heat, add the white chocolate and stir it in.

3. Remove to a steel bowl to cool. The mixture will thicken once it cools down.

Heston Blumenthal

Smoked Salmon with Soda
 Bread and Pickled Cucumber
Pot Roast Pork
Truffle Macaroni
Pears Poached in Red Wine

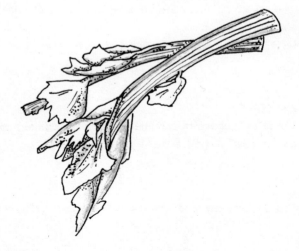

SMOKED SALMON WITH SODA BREAD AND PICKLED CUCUMBER

SERVES 8–12

1ST STAGE:
1 side organic salmon, pin boned and trimmed
2kg fine sea salt
1kg caster sugar
10g chopped fresh dill

METHOD

1. Mix the salt, sugar and dill together well.

2. Take either a plastic container longer, wider and deeper than the salmon, or a piece of tin foil twice the length and width of the salmon.

3. Sprinkle the base of the container/the tin foil with a handful of the salt; mix in a thin and even layer.

4. Lay the salmon on top then cover completely and evenly with the rest of the mix. This stage is absolutely vital to ensure an even cure on the salmon.

5. If using a plastic container, cover well with cling-film or tin foil; otherwise fold your piece of tin foil around the salmon to neatly cover it, then wrap the whole thing again in tin foil.

6. Leave to cure in the refrigerator for 36 hours.

2ND STAGE:
1–2 litres (enough to completely cover the salmon) good quality olive oil (not extra virgin)

METHOD

1. You will definitely need a plastic container or large sealable plastic

bag for this stage, so will hopefully have procured one in the previous 36 hours!

2. Take the salmon fillet and rinse off the salt mix well, then pat dry with paper towels.

3. Place the salmon into your container/bag and cover with the olive oil.

4. The salmon must be completely covered and the container/bag sealed to prevent oxidisation.

5. Leave the salmon in the oil for 24 hours.

3RD STAGE:
6 lots of 40g woodchips
6 Lapsang Souchong teabags

SMOKING SET UP:
1 deep metal tray
1 shallower, perforated metal tray (to slot into deep tray)
4 small saucepans
wire rack, to fit inside metal trays
tin foil
ice

METHOD

1. Take salmon out of oil and wipe off any excess.

2. Take all smoking equipment outside.

3. Take 2 saucepans and put 40g woodchips and 1 teabag in each and set alight.

4. Whilst the woodchips are starting to flame, put ice into the other two saucepans.

5. Once the chips are burning really well, extinguish by covering the pans with a lid.

6. Place the smoking chips into the deep metal tray, then place a perforated tray on top.

7. Put the 2 pans of ice on this perforated tray, followed by the wire rack, upon which you place your salmon.

8. For the smoker to work, all the smoke must be contained; wrap the whole thing in tin foil (or a box if you have one large enough to cover it)

9. Leave to smoke for 45 minutes, then repeat the above process twice more.

4TH STAGE:

1. Remove the salmon from the smoker and wrap in muslin cloth.

2. Refrigerate for 24 hours to complete maturation.

3. Slice salmon lengthways and serve with soda bread and pickled cucumber.

SODA BREAD
300g whole-wheat flour
50g fine oatmeal
20g butter
1 tsp bicarbonate of soda
½ tsp fine sea salt
1 tsp caster sugar
250g buttermilk at 60°C
150g whole milk at 60°C

METHOD

1. Preheat the over to 210°C/Gas mark 6.

2. Grease a 17cm square tin with butter then dust lightly with flour.

3. Mix the flour and oatmeal then rub in the butter.

4. Add bicarbonate soda, salt and sugar and mix with your fingers.

5. Combine milk and buttermilk then add to the flour mix.

6. Mix well, ensuring all ingredients are well incorporated.

7. Place the dough into the tin.

8. Pat the dough down to form an even layer and cover the tin with tin foil.

9. Bake for 25 minutes, remove tin foil then bake for a further 25 minutes.

10. Allow to cool slightly in the tin, then tip out onto a wire rack.

11. Once cool, wrap in wax paper to store or freeze in an airtight container.

PICKLED CUCUMBER

1 cucumber
50g sugar
100g white wine vinegar
150ml water
2 tsp chopped dill
6g salt

METHOD

1. Slice the cucumber 3mm thick on a mandolin.

2. Bring the sugar, wine vinegar and water to the boil.

3. Allow to cool and add the cucumber slices.

4. Leave the cucumber in the pickle 24 hours before using.

5. The cucumbers will begin to lose their colour after 3 days; if making to keep, peel the cucumbers first and keep the pickle in an airtight container in the fridge.

6. To serve, drain slices of cucumber and sprinkle with a little extra dill and fleur de sel.

POT ROAST PORK

SERVES 4

1 x 4-rib rack of pork (free range if possible) taken 2 ribs
back from the best end (just ask your butcher)
a little salt and pepper

FOR THE CURE:
200g salt
1 large bunch of thyme
1 clove of garlic
1 bunch of sage
salt and pepper

FOR THE GLAZE:
3 egg yolks
2 tbsp honey
2 tbsp Indonesian soy sauce

FOR THE COOKING PROCESS:
1 large onion
2 medium-large carrots
1 leek
3 cloves of garlic
1 bunch of thyme
1 bunch of marjoram (optional)
150g unsalted butter
50ml groundnut oil

METHOD

Two or three days in advance:

1. Chop the thyme leaves and mix them with the salt, reserve.

2. Peel the garlic and cut into matchstick thick batons, making sure
that you have at least 18 of them.

3. Blanch these in water for one minute, drain and refresh. Repeat this process twice and pat dry.

4. Put some salt and freshly ground pepper in a small ramekin in the proportions of approximately 1 teaspoon salt to ¼ teaspoon of pepper and drop the garlic batons in this mix.

5. Mix well then wrap each one in a small sage leaf. Reserve.

6. Now, take the piece of pork and turn it upside down so that you are looking at the flat, bony side.

7. With a small pointed knife, make two parallel rows of incisions, about 1½ cm deep, and insert into each one a sage wrapped garlic baton.

8. Still working on the same side, make three similar incisions in the fat that connects the skin to the meat, inserting the garlic as before.

9. Now turn the rack so that you are looking down on the ribs and again make two rows of holes, in between each rib.

10. Stuff these as before.

11. Finally, turn the rack so that it is sitting on its flat side and you are now looking down onto the top of the bones. Make the last three incisions into the fat that runs alongside the skin.

12. This process is far easier than it sounds; the important thing here is to get 18 sage wrapped batons into the meat evenly without sticking them deep into the meat, but rather into the fat or against the bone.

13. Now on your work surface, lay out some cling film, big enough to wrap around the pork twice and cover an area about the same size as the meat with about half of the herbed salt.

14. Place the pork skin side down onto the salt and cover all of the sides except for the exposed meat ends with the rest of the salt then carefully wrap the joint twice in the cling film. Make sure that the salt stays in position.

15. Place in the fridge.

16. After two days, thoroughly wash off the salt and pat dry the meat.

On the day of cooking:

1. Peel and quarter the onion and carrots, cut the root and green top off the leek and cut into four lengths.

2. Preheat the oven to 170°C/Gas mark 3.

3. In a lidded casserole big enough to fit the joint, melt 100g butter with the groundnut oil over a moderate heat.

4. When beginning to colour, add the pork and lightly brown on all sides. This browning process is important as it will give a stronger, richer flavour to the sauce.

5. Remove the pork and, if necessary, replace the butter if too brown.

6. Now lightly colour the vegetables and place the pork on top, skin side down.

7. Add the herbs, put the lid on and place in the oven.

8. After about 25 minutes, remove the casserole, turn the pork over and return to the oven for another 25 minutes.

9. Remove the casserole from the oven, take out the pork and put onto a chopping board.

10. Turn the oven up to 220°C/Gas mark 7.

11. With a sharp knife, carefully remove the skin taking care to leave as much fat on the meat as possible. Score this fat by running a knife through it in a criss-cross pattern, ensuring that you do not go into the meat itself and allow the meat to rest until you have made the sauce.

To make the sauce:

1. Place the casserole on a moderate heat and allow the vegetables to caramelise to a lovely golden brown.

2. Pour out the excess fat.

3. Add about 300ml cold water, bring to the boil and simmer for 20 minutes.

4. Strain this into a smaller pan and, if necessary, reduce a little to the desired consistency, set aside.

To make the glaze:

1. Whisk all the ingredients together.

To finish the dish, generously brush the fat with the glaze and return the pork to the hot oven until nicely caramelised. This should take approximately 10 minutes. You can, if you wish, put the skin in the oven for crackling. When ready, remove the pork from the oven and put onto a carving board. With a long, sharp knife, cut down and across against the contour of the bone to leave just the joint of meat.

Collect any juices that may have come out of the meat and add to the sauce. Finish this with a knob of butter, gently whisking it in.

At the table, cut the pork into thick slices and serve with some truffle macaroni (see next page) or traditional veg, potatoes and all the trimmings.

TRUFFLE MACARONI

SERVES 4

200ml double cream
100ml truffle juice
150ml brown chicken stock
100g Macaroni (Di Cecco, type Zita)
10g salt
1 litre boiling water
salt and pepper
truffle oil

METHOD

1. Reduce the stock, truffle juice and cream in separate pans.
2. Mix together and season.
3. In another pan, add the salt to the water and bring to a boil.
4. Cook the pasta three-quarters of the way, then drain and cut into 1cm pieces.
5. Add the pasta to the sauce and return to the heat.
6. Cook until the sauce begins to thicken and come together.
7. Season and add truffle oil to taste.

PEARS POACHED IN RED WINE

These pears are always best made a day or two in advance. If they are eaten too soon, the poaching liquid will only have penetrated into some of the flesh, the centre part still being white.

If you do not have any Crème de Cassis, substitute it with the same amount of blackcurrant syrup or, failing that, add an extra 100g of sugar to the liquid. As regards the wine, remember the saying; 'If it is not good enough to drink, do not cook with it'. The ginger and liquorice are optional. If you are using liquorice make sure that it is the root and not the confectionery. If the poaching liquid is a little thin, simply thicken it with a little cornflour.

You have a choice when preparing the pears; personally, I think that they look nicer left whole, however, they are slightly more fiddly to prepare. If you haven't got the inclination to do this, you can just cut them in half. You will need a casserole large enough to fit the pears in one layer. You may have to adjust the quantities accordingly, depending on how many pears you will fit in the pan.

SERVES 4–8

8–10 ripe and unblemished pears (allow 1–2 pears per person depending on their size)
1 bottle red wine
200ml Crème de cassis or blackcurrant syrup
200g sugar (300g if neither of the above)
1 cinnamon stick
6 cloves
1 star anise
20g ginger root
2 liquorice sticks
zest of 1 orange and 1 lemon

METHOD

1. Bring the wine to a boil, flame it to reduce some of its acidity and add all the other ingredients.

2. Meanwhile prepare the pears.

3. Peel them whether you will be halving them or not.

4. If keeping them whole, you will need to remove the core so that they will cook evenly the whole way through. To do this, insert the tip of a normal peeler into the base of the pear, just on the edge of the core, push it into the fruit and turning the peeler around the core, cut it out.

5. If halving the pears, do so lengthways and again, use the tip of the peeler to cut out the root and the core.

6. The liquid will have cooled down a little. Place the pears side by side and top with a disk, the diameter of the pan, of greaseproof paper with holes pierced in it.

7. Press down slightly so that some of the poaching liquid comes through the holes made in the paper, keeping the pears submerged during the cooking. If the liquid does not cover the pears, add a little water until it does.

8. Place the casserole back on the heat and bring the liquid to a simmer.

9. As soon as this happens, turn the heat down and cook at a very gentle simmer, just enough to form the odd bubble on the surface of the water.

10. Cook until the pears are done; you can test this by inserting a small pointed knife into the flesh. If it goes in with little resistance, they are ready.

11. Remove the pan from the heat and leave to cool.

12. When cold, carefully transfer the fruit to a sealable container. If you have added some extra water now reduce the liquid to the required consistency and taste.

13. Pour the liquid over the pears in their container and store in the fridge for at least one day. The pears will keep for a week in the poaching liquid.

14. Serve hot or cold and adjust the consistency of the liquid as required.

Paul Bocuse

Boiled Artichokes
Pot-au-Feu
Rice Custard

BOILED ARTICHOKES

SERVES 4

4 artichokes
4 litres water
2 tbsp coarse salt
1 tbsp Dijon mustard
3 tbsp red wine vinegar
9 tbsp walnut oil
salt and pepper

METHOD

1. Choose only artichokes that are firm and green, not bruised or discoloured from shipping. Cook them in an enamelled or stainless steel pot to avoid discolouration.

2. Bring the water and salt to a boil.

3. Cut off the stem of each artichoke, then rinse in hot water before placing them in the pot to cook. The artichokes should simmer, not boil, for 40 minutes.

4. When done, lift them out of the pot and place them, leaves down, next to the sink to drain.

5. Make an oil and vinegar dressing by combing the mustard, vinegar, walnut oil and a little salt and pepper.

6. Serve the artichokes warm, with the dressing, in small individual bowls.

POT-AU-FEU

SERVES 8 OR MORE

200g steak bones
1.5kg beef shanks
500g beef ribs
500g flank steak
500g chuck steak
500g ox tail
500g veal shanks
about 1.5kg poultry
5 marrow bones, about 3cm in length
500g sirloin steak
300g leeks
300g carrots
2 celery heads
300g round turnips
1 whole fennel bulb
1 parsnip
1 whole head of garlic
bouquet garni, made with bay leaves, parsley, chervil, thyme
and green leek leaves
250g onions, studded with cloves
3 large tomatoes, peeled and chopped
coarse salt
peppercorns
pickles, mustard and toasted bread (for serving)

METHOD

1. Take a large stew-pot and place the steak bones at the bottom.

2. Then place in order: the beef shanks, the ribs, the flank steak, the chuck steak, the ox tail, and finally the veal shanks.

PAUL BOCUSE

43

3. Add cold water so that the meat is completely covered.

4. Do not season with salt immediately.

5. Cook over a high heat without covering.

6. While the meat is cooking, peel the vegetables.

7. Wash them with boiling water.

8. Prepare the bouquet garni by tying together bay leaves, parsley, chervil, thyme, and green leek leaves.

9. Wrap the marrow bones in muslin.

10. After the meat has cooked for 20 minutes, use a ladle to skim off all the foam that has gathered at the surface of the bouillon.

11. Lower the heat and allow to cook for another 20 minutes.

12. Add the peppercorns.

13. Place in the poultry after trussing it.

14. Then add the bouquet garni and the onions studded with cloves.

15. Add the garlic, the leeks tied in a bundle and all the vegetables except the tomatoes.

16. Skim once again, then allow to simmer for one hour.

17. Season with salt.

18. Take out the vegetables gradually as they cook, checking whether they are ready with the help of a pointed knife or kitchen needle.

19. Keep the vegetables warm, dousing them with two ladlefuls of bouillon.

20. Take out the poultry as soon as it is cooked, keeping it warm in the same way as the vegetables, by placing the vessel containing the vegetables and poultry on the stove at a low temperature.

21. Allow the meat to cook for another 30 minutes, skimming the bouillon from time to time, then remove the veal shanks, which should be kept warm with the poultry.

22. Allow the remaining meats to cook gently for another hour.

23. Add the sirloin, the marrow bones and the tomatoes. Do not forget to skim.

24. Allow the sirloin to cook for between 15 and 20 minutes, depending on its thickness.

25. Remove the remaining meats and arrange them on the serving platter.

26. To warm up the meats taken out first, immerse them in the bouillon for 5 minutes then arrange them on the platter along with the vegetables and marrow bones.

27. Serve at the table with coarse sea salt, black pepper, pickles and mustard. Serve the bouillon in side bowls accompanied by toasted bread.

28. To embellish the meat and vegetables, you can also prepare a simple sauce made up of a soupspoonful of wine vinegar, four soup spoonfuls of walnut oil, sea salt, ground black pepper, and two soup spoonfuls of shredded chervil.

29. Leftovers from the Pot-au-Feu can be used for different dishes in the days to follow — hachis Parmentier, stuffed tomatoes, jellied beef etc.

RICE CUSTARD

SERVES 4–6

1 litre milk
200g granulated sugar
½ tsp salt
1 vanilla bean, split in half lengthways
200g rice

METHOD

1. Place the milk, sugar, salt and vanilla bean in a large saucepan and bring to a boil.

2. Sprinkle in the rice, stirring.

3. Lower the heat (use a heat diffuser for very low, even heat) and cook the rice for 45 minutes to 1 hour, or until it is tender and has absorbed practically all of the milk (the milk left over will be absorbed as the rice cools).

4. Remove the vanilla bean, pour the rice into a bowl and leave it to cool. It can be served either hot or cold.

Serving Suggestion:

Serve with homemade jam, poached fruit or candied fruits.

Clare Clark

Deluxe Coffee Ice Cream
Chocolate Fudge Brownies
Lemon Posset

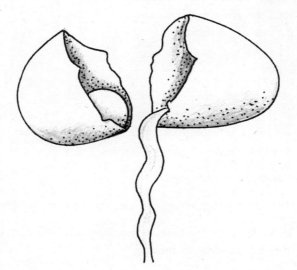

DELUXE COFFEE ICE CREAM

The quality of the coffee is critical to the overall taste and flavour of the ice cream. Use only whole coffee beans and grind them yourself or have the shop grind them for you. Ready ground beans, the type you get at a good quality coffee house that are sealed in foil bags for freshness, are also very good. I use espresso beans as they have a bitter, sharp taste that complements the richness and creaminess of the ice cream base.

SERVES 4

500ml milk plus extra as needed
500ml double cream
3 tbsp ground espresso beans
12 egg yolks
250g caster sugar

FOR THE GARNISH:
300g tempered white chocolate
300g tempered dark chocolate
1 A4 sheet of plastic

METHOD

1. Bring the milk and cream to the boil with the ground coffee. As soon as it boils, turn off the heat and let the coffee infuse in the mix for 10 minutes. Return to the heat and bring back to the boil, then let the coffee infuse another 10 minutes.

2. Pass through a fine strainer.

3. After straining the coffee mix, measure the contents of the pan.

4. Make the coffee mix back up to 1 litre with extra milk. Return to a clean pan and bring to the boil.

5. Combine the egg yolks with the sugar and mix well. Pour the strained boiled coffee mix over the combined eggs and sugar, stir and return to the pan.

6. Cook over a low heat, stirring continuously, until the mix coats the back of a spoon or reaches 86°C. Do not allow the mix to boil or it will split and separate.

7. Pass immediately through a fine strainer into a bowl. Place the bowl over another bowl full of ice to prevent the custard from cooking further.

8. Cool completely then churn in an ice cream machine.

9. Serve with chocolate sauce or crème anglaise and decorate with two-toned chocolate décor.

For the Chocolate Décor:

The décor will keep for 4–6 weeks stored on a tray and wrapped in the fridge. Make more than you need and use it to decorate cakes and desserts.

Use overhead projector sheets of film to make the chocolate décor on. It is the perfect thickness and size.

Randomly drizzle the dark chocolate from a fork or the back of a spoon over the plastic sheet to make the pattern of your choice. Let the dark chocolate set. Spoon several tablespoons of the tempered white chocolate onto the same sheet of plastic over the dark chocolate and spread with a palette knife until it is smooth and thin. Let the sheet of chocolate set then place it on a tray. Wrap the tray and set in the fridge. Break off shards of décor and use as required.

CHOCOLATE FUDGE BROWNIES

I thought hard about which recipe I should use for this book. I have several I use when compiling different dishes, however I have chosen the recipe I actually like the best to eat simply as a brownie, plus it is versatile enough to double up as a base for a dessert if you should so wish. One of my favourite brownie desserts consists of chocolate brownie cubes, butterscotch sauce, velvet white chocolate mousse and lots of dark chocolate shavings and whipped cream, and possibly a little hot chocolate sauce too.

SERVES 8–12

280g dark 70% chocolate
3 large eggs
10ml vanilla extract
280g dark brown sugar
80g plain flour, sifted
8g baking powder
pinch of salt
200g butter, melted
200g pecan nuts

1 x 18cm x 25cm oblong cake pan

METHOD

1. Preheat the oven to 170°C/Gas mark 3.

2. Take half the chocolate and melt it in a bowl over a pan of water. As soon as it is melted remove the bowl from over the pan and leave on the stove top to keep warm.

3. Chop the remaining chocolate into small pieces.

4. Whisk the eggs, vanilla and sugar in a mixer bowl with a whisk attachment until pale and doubled in volume.

5. Remove from the machine and fold in the sieved flour, baking powder, and salt. Combine the melted chocolate and butter and fold into the mix.

6. Lastly, add the chopped chocolate and pecan nuts. Mix well.

7. Transfer to the lined baking pan and bake at 170°C/Gas mark 3 for approx 30–40 minutes. Check with a cake skewer to see if it comes out clean. Do not over-bake the brownies as they are best soft and chewy.

8. Cool in the tin and cut into squares.

CC's Tips:

Serve warm with homemade vanilla ice cream.

Make sure the butter and melted chocolate are both warm when you add them to the mix.

Use good quality vanilla extract, it makes all the difference. If you can find extract with seeds in it then buy it.

LEMON POSSET

The non-complexity of this recipe yields a surprisingly decadent, smooth and silky crème.

SERVES 4–6

4 unwaxed leafy lemons
250g caster sugar
500ml double cream

FOR THE DECORATION:
candied lemon peel strips
pistachio nuts or flaked almonds
icing sugar

METHOD

1. Juice the lemons and strain.

2. Place the strained juice in a pan with the caster sugar. Bring to the boil over a low heat, stirring continuously until the sugar has dissolved. Keep this warm on the side of the stove.

3. In a separate heavy bottomed pan, boil the cream. Once the cream has boiled pour over the lemon and sugar mix.

4. Whisk gently to combine the ingredients. Pass the mixture through a fine sieve into a measuring jug.

5. Pour into individual serving dishes. Chill in the fridge for 2 hours until set.

6. Decorate with the lemon peel and pistachio nuts or toasted flaked almonds and a little icing sugar.

Sam and Sam Clark

Leek and Yoghurt Soup
Fish Tagine with Potatoes,
 Tomatoes and Olives
Malaga Raisin Ice Cream

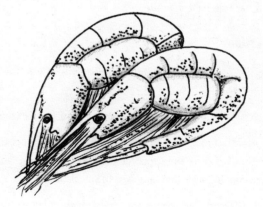

Here are three of our favourite recipes — one from Turkey, one from Morocco and one from Spain. We hope, like much of the food we cook, that the taste of each dish has the power to transport you to another time and another place. Bon voyage!

LEEK AND YOGHURT SOUP

SERVES 4

50g butter
3 tbsp olive oil
4 medium leeks, trimmed, cut in half lengthways, washed,
drained and thinly sliced
1 tsp chilli flakes or paprika
1 rounded tsp dried mint or 2 tsp finely chopped fresh mint
1 egg
½ tbsp plain flour or cornflour
350g Greek yoghurt
500ml water, chicken or vegetable stock
75g unsalted butter, heated over a low heat, stirring
occasionally, until the white whey turns golden brown and has
a caramelised aroma.

METHOD

1. Place a large saucepan over a medium heat and add the butter and olive oil.

2. When the butter begins to foam, stir in the leeks.

3. After 10 minutes add the chilli flakes or paprika and mint and continue to cook the leeks for another 20–30 minutes, stirring occasionally until they are sweet. Set aside.

4. In a large bowl, whisk the egg with the flour until a smooth paste is formed. This will stabilise the yoghurt when it is heated. Now stir in the yoghurt and thin with the water or stock.

5. Pour onto the leeks and return the saucepan to the heat.

6. Gently heat the soup over a low to medium heat, stirring every now and then.

7. Do not allow the soup to boil, but remove from the heat just before it bubbles.

8. The soup should have a smooth silky quality, and be the consistency of single cream.

9. Check for seasoning and pour the caramelised butter on top.

FISH TAGINE WITH POTATOES, TOMATOES AND OLIVES

SERVES 4

4 hake steaks about 225–250g each or 4 fillets of monkfish or
any other firmish white fish, about 200g each
20 small, waxy new potatoes, peeled
3 tbsp olive oil
2 garlic cloves
15 cherry tomatoes, halved
3 large green peppers, grilled until black and blistered,
skinned, seeded and sliced into strips
a handful of black oily olives
100ml water

FOR THE CHARMOULA:
2 garlic cloves
1 level tsp sea salt
2 tsp freshly ground cumin
juice of 1 lemon
½ tbsp good quality red wine vinegar
1 tsp paprika
1 small bunch fresh coriander, roughly chopped
1 tbsp olive oil

METHOD

1. We make the charmoula, the classic Moroccan marinade, in a
mortar and pestle. Pound the garlic with the salt until a smooth
paste is formed, then add the cumin followed by the lemon juice,
vinegar, paprika, coriander and olive oil. Rub two-thirds of the
charmoula mixture into the fish and stand it in the fridge for
between 20 minutes and 2 hours.

2. Boil the potatoes in salted water for 10–15 minutes until just tender. Drain and halve lengthways.

3. In a medium saucepan, heat 2 tablespoons of the olive oil over a medium heat and fry the garlic until light brown.

4. Add the tomatoes and toss for 2 minutes until they begin to soften.

5. Stir in the green peppers and remaining charmoula and check for seasoning.

6. In a 25cm tagine, saucepan or frying pan with a lid, spread the potatoes evenly over the bottom.

7. Scatter three quarters of the pepper and tomato mixture over the potatoes then place the marinated fish on top.

8. Dab a little of the remaining pepper and tomato on top of each fish as well as the olives. Add the water, drizzle on the remaining tablespoon of olive oil, put on the lid and steam over a medium to high heat for 10–15 minutes or until the fish is cooked through.

The beauty of this dish is that it hardly needs anything to accompany it, perhaps just a little salad and some bread.

MALAGA RAISIN ICE CREAM

Although a very simple recipe using a basic custard for the ice-cream, all the complexity and flavour comes from the sherry. The raisins are soaked in Pedro Ximenez sherry, the treacly, sweet, raisiny sherry made from Pedro Ximenez grapes, that are first dried in the sun to concentrate their sugar and flavour.

SERVES 8 (MAKES JUST OVER A LITRE)

600ml double cream
300ml milk
1 small cinnamon stick
1 vanilla pod
7 egg yolks
85g caster sugar
100g raisins covered with 100ml Pedro Ximenez sherry or Pedro Ximenez Malaga wine

METHOD

1. Place the cream, milk and cinnamon stick in a large saucepan.

2. Split the vanilla pod in half lengthways and scrape the tiny seeds into the pan. Heat until just below boiling point then remove from the stove and strain.

3. Beat the egg yolks and sugar together for 5–10 minutes until pale and thick.

4. Loosen the egg with a little of the cream/milk mixture, then pour the egg mixture into the saucepan, scraping the bowl out with a spatula.

5. Whisk well to mix everything properly and return to a low heat, stirring constantly.

6. Heat gently to cook out the egg but be careful not to curdle the custard.

7. When the mixture thickens and just before it bubbles, remove from the heat, pour into a bowl and place over ice water to cool.

8. Churn in an ice cream machine (in batches if necessary) adding the raisins and sherry towards the end of the churning.

9. For those without an ice cream machine, try freezing the ice cream by hand, but remember to stir every half hour to prevent crystallisation. Stirring will also help to distribute the raisins evenly as they tend to sink to the bottom before the custard hardens enough to support them. This process will take about 2 hours, depending on the temperature of your freezer.

10. Serve with a chilled glass of Pedro Ximenez on the side or poured over the ice cream.

Sally Clarke

Wild Mushrooms...
Pot Roasted Pigeon...
Parmesan Polenta
Spiced Apple and Prune
  Strudel

WILD MUSHROOMS BAKED IN CREAM WITH GORGONZOLA MASCARPONE

My mother is the best golfer I know, but in the autumn months her game goes seriously downhill. I am sure that she hits the balls into the woods on purpose though, because more often than not she can be found emerging from the bushes with her golf bag filled to the brim with ceps, bay boletus, hedgehog mushrooms and other forms of fungi.

Once home, we trim them together, eliminating any maggots, and then I ask one of the restaurant's official wild mushroom suppliers to verify their authenticity. We then place them on the menus in recipes such as this. Its flavours speak volumes to me of why this season is so special.

NB. Do not attempt to search for and cook your own mushrooms unless you know a mushroom expert who is able to authenticate your harvest for you. Alternatively, make a study of one of the authorised books on the subject (see *A Passion for Mushrooms* by Antonio Carluccio or *Mushrooms and other Fungi of Great Britain and Europe* by Roger Phillips).

SERVES 4

600g wild mushrooms, brushed and trimmed of discoloured parts
50g butter
2 garlic cloves, crushed to a cream with salt
salt and pepper
2 tbsp chopped Italian flat leafed parsley, and 6 sprigs for garnish
2 tsp chopped fresh rosemary, and 6 sprigs for garnish
450ml double cream
60g Gorgonzola mascarpone

METHOD

1. Preheat the oven to 180°C/Gas mark 4.

2. Cut the mushrooms into large even-sized pieces.

3. Heat the butter in a heavy-based non-stick frying pan, add the garlic and when sizzling add the mushrooms.

4. Toss over a high heat and cook until almost tender.

5. Season with salt, pepper, parsley and rosemary and remove with a slotted spoon to an ovenproof dish.

6. To the remaining juices in the pan add the cream and reduce by a third.

7. Taste for seasoning and pour over the mushrooms.

8. Bake for 10–15 minutes or until the cream has bubbled and started to brown at the edges.

9. Scoop Gorgonzola mascarpone into walnut sized pieces, dot it over the mushrooms and allow it to melt as it is served.

10. Garnish with sprigs of parsley and rosemary.

SALLY CLARKE

POT-ROASTED PIGEON WITH PARMESAN POLENTA AND WHITE TRUFFLE

SERVES 6

6 squab pigeon
salt and pepper
3 tsp chopped thyme leaves
3 large carrots, peeled
1 large onion
4 sticks celery
1 fennel bulb
60g unsalted butter
1 head garlic, roughly chopped
½ litre hearty red wine
½ litre dark chicken stock or game stock
4 bay leaves
a sprig each of rosemary, thyme and sage

METHOD

1. Preheat the oven to 180°C/Gas mark 4

2. Trim the wing tips, neck end and parson's nose from the pigeons and dry the cavities with kitchen paper. Season the cavities with salt, pepper and thyme.

3. Chop the carrot, onion, celery and fennel into hazelnut-sized pieces.

4. In a large heavy-based pan over a medium heat, warm a third of the butter until sizzling. Place the pigeons in the pan, breast-side down, and turn them occasionally until the skin turns golden, about 8–10 minutes.

5. Remove the pigeons to one side and add half the remaining butter to the pan.

6. Over a high heat, cook the diced vegetables and garlic until golden brown, stirring occasionally to scrape the residue from the bottom of the pan.

7. Arrange the pigeons breast-side up on top of the vegetables, season with a little extra salt and pepper and add the wine, stock, bay leaves and sprigs of herbs and bring to the boil. The liquid does not have to cover the birds completely.

8. Put a lid on the pan and place it in the oven. Cook for at least 25–35 minutes or until a skewer moves without resistance through the thigh meat.

9. Remove the pigeons to a deep platter and cover with foil to keep them warm.

10. Place the pan over a high heat and reduce the liquid by half, skimming frequently to remove any fat or scum which may rise to the surface.

11. Strain the juices into a clean pan and taste for seasoning. Heat to a gentle simmer and stir in the remaining butter. Pour over the pigeons and serve with soft parmesan polenta.

PARMESAN POLENTA

SERVES 6

700ml water
salt and black pepper
2 tsp chopped thyme leaves
150g medium-ground polenta
50g unsalted butter
100g freshly grated Parmesan

TO SERVE:
1 white truffle, approx. 30g (optional), brushed clean

METHOD

1. Bring the water to the boil in a heavy-based pan with the salt, pepper and half the thyme.

2. Pour the polenta into the pan slowly and gently, whisking it continuously until it becomes smooth.

3. With a wooden spoon, continue to stir it over a low heat as it thickens. This will take up to 15 minutes, during which time the polenta will cook through.

4. Remove from the heat and add the butter, the remaining thyme and half the Parmesan.

5. Serve sprinkled with the remaining Parmesan and shavings of white truffle if using.

SPICED APPLE AND PRUNE STRUDEL

SERVES 6–8

900g Bramley apples
300g eating apples, such as Cox's, Jonagold or Spartan
12 pitted prunes, soaked overnight in the juice of 2 oranges
zest of 1 lemon
zest of 1 orange
150g sultanas or raisins
75g Demerara sugar or 2 tbsp runny honey
2 tsp mixed spice
a pinch of ground black pepper
6 sheets of frozen or fresh filo pastry
50g butter, melted

TO SERVE:
250ml double cream, whipped

METHOD

1. Peel and core all the apples and cut them into walnut sized pieces.

2. Place them in a bowl with all the remaining ingredients except the filo pastry and butter. Toss gently together and leave on one side.

3. Preheat the oven to 190°C /Gas mark 5.

4. Unroll the filo pastry and check that all sheets are unbroken. Cover with a cloth to prevent them from drying. Brush a baking sheet with a little of the butter.

5. Lay a clean tea towel short side towards you on the work surface and lay a sheet of pastry on top, long side towards you.

6. Brush with a little butter and place the next sheet on top of half the first sheet, increasing the depth.

SALLY CLARKE

67

7. Brush again with butter.

8. Place the third sheet over the area covered by the first sheet and continue layering and buttering as before.

9. Using a slotted spoon, pile the fruit along the length of the front edge making sure that the prunes are evenly distributed.

10. Lift up the front edge of the tea towel gently and carefully but firmly begin to roll the pastry around the apple into a sausage shape, tucking in the ends to prevent the apple from falling out.

11. Just before reaching the far end, brush the final 2cm of filo pastry with butter and press the roll over this to seal it well.

12. With the aid of the tea towel lift the strudel onto the baking sheet and bake for approximately 30 minutes or until crisp and golden.

13. Serve warm or chilled the following day with lots of whipped cream.

Anthony Demetre

Squid and Mackerel Burger
Cod, Braised Gem and Sea
  Kale, Parsley Juice
Floating Island with Pink
  Pralines

SQUID AND MACKEREL 'BURGER', SEA PURSLANE, PARSLEY JUICE

SERVES 6

2 medium mackerel, filleted
200g squid – frozen to tenderise, cleaned and trimmed
1 tbsp chopped fresh coriander
1 tbsp grated fresh ginger
1 tbsp chopped garlic
1 tsp lime zest
salt and pepper
olive oil
sesame oil
sea purslane
50g whole young chipiron (baby squid)
1 bunch parsley

METHOD

1. Finely chop the fish, add the herbs and aromatics, season with salt and pepper and mix well. Leave to set for 2 hours in the fridge.

2. Mould into 100g burgers with the aid of cling film.

3. Pan fry in half olive and half sesame oil until cooked through and golden.

4. Sauté the young squid in the same mix of oils.

5. For the parsley sauce, blanch the parsley in salted water, refresh in cold water, and blitz it with a little hot water.

6. Garnish the burgers with the sautéed squid and the sea purslane and serve with a drizzle of parsley sauce.

COD, BRAISED GEM AND SEA KALE, PARSLEY JUICE

SERVES 4

4 portions of Icelandic cod
4 sprigs of rosemary
4 young gem lettuce
1 bunch Scottish sea kale
unsalted butter
olive oil
lemon juice
salt and pepper
1 bunch parsley

METHOD

1. Roast the cod in butter with a sprig of rosemary.

2. Season with salt and pepper and a squeeze of lemon juice towards the end of cooking.

3. Split the baby gem lettuce, wash and dry.

4. Colour in a knob of butter and a splash of olive oil.

5. Add a splash of water, cover and cook for 10 minutes in a moderate oven.

6. Cut the sea kale to desired size and cook until tender in half butter, half water, a splash of lemon juice and seasoning.

7. Blanch the parsley in plenty of salted water, refresh in cold water.

8. Liquidise the parsley with the juices from the gem and kale.

9. Serve.

ANTHONY DEMETRE

FLOATING ISLAND WITH PINK PRALINES

SERVES 6

6 egg whites
300g caster sugar
Pink Pralines
6 egg yolks
375ml whole milk
75g caster sugar
1 vanilla pod, split

METHOD

1. Whip the egg whites until they form soft peaks, add the sugar and continue whipping until the peaks are fairly stiff.

2. Fold in chopped pink pralines, and mould meringues to desired shape.

3. Poach gently in the milk until set, remove and leave to cool.

4. Infuse the poaching milk with the vanilla pod, then strain.

5. Prepare custard in the usual way with the egg yolks, sugar and infused milk.

6. Finally, sprinkle over some extra chopped pink praline.

NOTE

Pink pralines are available from La Fromagerie, London, www.lafromagerie.co.uk.

Alain Ducasse

Fruit and Vegetable
  Casserole
Langoustine Gratin
Brioche slices with
  Fruit Compote

FRUIT AND VEGETABLE CASSEROLE

SERVES 4

1 small cabbage heart
300g salsify
1 small Swiss chard
2 Roseval potatoes
2 apples
2 pears
4 small carrots
4 small turnips
4 poivrade artichokes (the small purple ones)
4 white onions
4 large strips of pork belly
100ml veal stock
20g goose fat
20g butter
20cl olive oil

TO SERVE:
1 fennel heart
1 celery heart
16 black grapes

METHOD

1. Blanch the cabbage, then cut into 8. Peel and rinse the salsify. Separate the leaves from the spine of the Swiss chard. Cook the 3 vegetables separately in salted water.

2. Wash the potatoes, cut in half and roast in the goose fat.

3. Core the apples with a corer and cut into thick rings. Cut the pears into 4 and remove the core. Fry the apples and pears in butter until both sides are golden brown.

4. Peel the carrots and turnips. Remove the tough leaves from the artichokes and cut into four. Quarter the onions.

5. Heat the oil in a large cast iron casserole dish and gently fry the artichokes. Put them to one side, then gradually fry the carrots, turnips and onions until golden brown. Remove and set aside.

6. Cut the pork into strips and brown them in the casserole. Pour in the stock and add back the vegetables. Add the cabbage, salsify and green and white parts of the Swiis chard. Simmer for 20 minutes until tender. Add the apple and pear and gently heat through for a few minutes.

7. Just before serving, grate the fennel and celery over the vegetables. Garnish with peeled grapes and serve.

LANGOUSTINE GRATIN

SERVES 4

24 large langoustines
3 garlic cloves
4 sprigs flat-leaf parsley
2 tbsp oil
2 tbsp cognac
salt and pepper
300ml dry white wine (such as an Aligoté from Burgundy)
½ tbsp mignonette pepper
5 tbsp very cold whipping cream
4 egg yolks
6 tbsp melted butter + more to grease the pans
juice of ½ lemon

METHOD

1. Wash the langoustines and twist the central part of each tail fin, pulling it off and taking the black vein with it. Detach the heads from the tails. Crush the garlic cloves without peeling them. Wash the parsley, pat it dry, and chop it.

2. Heat 1 tablespoon oil in a Le Creuset saucepan. Sauté the langoustine tails over high heat for 2 minutes. Remove the pot from the heat; add the garlic cloves and parsley. Cover with a damp cloth and leave to infuse for 15 minutes.

3. Remove the langoustine tails and empty the saucepan. Heat 1 tablespoon oil and sauté the tails again over high heat until they are very firm. Add the cognac and set it alight. When the flames are extinguished, scrape the bottom of the pot with a wooden spatula to dissolve the sediment. Season with salt and generously with pepper. Cover the pot and remove from the heat.

4. Make a sabayon by reducing the white wine with the mignonette pepper until it becomes syrupy. Remove it from the heat. Whip the cream. Add the egg yolks to the reduced white wine. Season with salt and beat the mixture in a bowl over a saucepan of simmering water until the mixture thickens. Melt the butter and add it in two lots, beating well after each addition. Then add the lemon juice and whipped cream, stirring without beating.

5. Lightly butter 4 individual gratin dishes. Divide the langoustines and their cooking juices between the dishes and coat them with the sabayon custard. Slide dishes under the grill and grill for a few minutes, watching to ensure the custard does not burn.

You can also make this dish with shelled langoustines. Sauté them in butter with the garlic, deglaze with the cognac, cover and leave to infuse off the heat for 5 to 10 minutes. Then season generously with salt and pepper. Then all you have to do is make the sabayon custard.

BRIOCHE SLICES WITH FRUIT COMPOTE

SERVES 4

8 slices of stale brioche
2 apples
2 pears
50g raisins
200g sugar
100g butter
1 vanilla pod, cut widthways into two
50cl milk
2 eggs

METHOD

1. Peel the apples and pears and cut into large cubes. Wash the raisins. Heat the oven to 140°C/Gas mark 4.

2. Put half the sugar into a small, round casserole with 2 dessertspoons of water. Cook until it turns to a light caramel.

3. Stop the caramel cooking by adding 50g butter. Add the fruit and the raisins. Spilt one of the vanilla pod halves into two and grate one half over the fruit. Add the second half. Put in the oven and cook for 30 minutes. The fruit should be soft but retain its shape. Add a little water if necessary.

4. Bring the milk to the boil with 20g sugar and the other half of the vanilla pod, split. Remove from the heat. Infuse until the milk is completely cold.

5. Beat the eggs with 80g sugar. Dip the brioche slices into the milk, then into the beaten egg. Melt 50g butter in a non-stick frying pan. Once it starts to bubble, brown the slices lightly on both sides. Serve warm with the fruit on the side.

Vary the fruit according to the season. Serve with whipped cream or ice cream.

James and Emma Faulks

Lentils, Boiled Egg
  and Anchoïade
Roast and Braised Pheasant
  with Bacon and Chestnuts
Stuffed Prunes and Shortbread

LENTILS, BOILED EGG AND ANCHOÏADE

SERVES 4

FOR THE ANCHOÏADE:
150g anchovy fillets in oil, drained
3 cloves garlic
1 tsp thyme
10 large basil leaves
1½ tbsp Dijon mustard
1 tbsp red wine vinegar
½ tsp chopped fresh red chilli
500ml virgin olive oil
water as needed

FOR THE LENTILS:
250g Spanish brown lentils
1 carrot, thinly sliced
1 onion, thinly sliced
½ leek, thinly sliced
2 cloves garlic
1 stick celery
50ml olive oil
bouquet garni
salt and pepper

TO SERVE:
soft boiled eggs
olive oil toasts

METHOD

1. Blend all the ingredients for the anchoïade, apart from the olive oil.

2. Slowly add the oil in a thin stream with the blender motor running.

3. Add sufficient water to achieve a mayonnaise-like consistency. Set aside.

4. Sweat the vegetables and the garlic in the oil until softened.

5. Add the lentils and the bouquet garni.

6. Cover with water, bring to a boil and simmer until the lentils are tender. Season to taste.

7. Serve the lentils warm in a bowl with soft boiled eggs and the anchoïade spread on the toasts.

ROAST AND BRAISED PHEASANT WITH BACON AND CHESTNUTS

The pheasant season runs from 1st October until 1st February; however, birds are not usually available until the beginning of November. Young hen pheasants have finer flesh and are considered better eating than the cock.

SERVES 2

1 pheasant (hen if possible), cleaned and prepared
80g smoked streaky bacon lardons
1 carrot, sliced
1 medium onion, sliced
1 stick of celery, sliced
3 or 4 sprigs of thyme
2 cloves garlic, smashed
a dozen blanched and peeled chestnuts
1 bay leaf
100g butter
60ml Madeira
250ml good chicken stock

Greens to serve (we like to use Brussels sprout tops)

METHOD

1. Remove the legs from the bird.

2. Season and brown in half the butter in a flameproof casserole (a small Le Creuset is perfect).

3. Remove the legs, add the bacon to the casserole and brown.

4. Add the vegetables, thyme, garlic and chestnuts and sweat until softened, adding a little extra butter if necessary.

5. Add Madeira and stock and bring to a simmer.

6. Return the legs to the pot, fit the lid and cook in a low preheated oven at 120°C/Gas mark ½ for 1–1½ hours, until the meat begins to fall from the bone. (This part of the dish may be carried out a day or two in advance if time is short, the legs can then just be gently reheated when needed.)

7. Season the carcass with salt and pepper. Heat the remaining butter and a splash of olive oil in a heavy pan until foaming.

8. Brown the carcass until the skin turns golden.

9. Cook in a preheated oven at 220°C/Gas mark 7 for 15 minutes (20 minutes for a cock pheasant).

10. Remove from the oven and allow to rest for 10 minutes whilst blanching the greens and reheating the legs if necessary.

11. Remove the breasts from the carcass and serve with the casseroled legs and the greens.

STUFFED PRUNES AND SHORTBREAD

SERVES 4

FOR THE PRUNES:
12 large fresh prunes
2 tbsp honey
1 cinnamon stick
1 strip of orange zest
1 strip of lemon zest

FOR THE SHORTBREAD:
310g plain sifted flour
250g cold unsalted butter
60g corn flour
60g caster sugar
caster sugar for sprinkling

FOR THE STUFFING:
250ml full-cream milk
½ vanilla pod
2 egg yolks
75g caster sugar
25g custard powder
200ml double cream
50ml Armagnac

METHOD

1. Place the prunes in a pan, cover with water and add the honey.

2. Bring to the boil and simmer for 10 minutes.

3. Allow to cool, add the orange zest, lemon zest and cinnamon.
Leave overnight.

4. To make the shortbread, combine all the ingredients apart from

the sugar for sprinkling, mix using a paddle or an electric mixer until a dough forms.

5. Roll the dough out to a thickness of 5mm on greaseproof paper and refrigerate for 30 minutes.

6. Cut into rectangles and place onto fresh greaseproof paper.

7. Bake in the middle of a pre-heated oven at 170°C/Gas mark 4 for 12 minutes. Do not allow biscuits to colour.

8. Remove and sprinkle with caster sugar.

9. To make the stuffing, split the vanilla pod lengthways and scrape out the seeds.

10. Place seeds, pod and the milk in a saucepan and bring to the boil.

11. Whisk egg yolks, sugar and custard powder together in a bowl.

12. Pour 1/3 of the milk into the egg mixture, whisking continuously, then pour back into the saucepan with the remaining milk.

13. Heat the mixture, whisking continuously, until thickened.

14. Pour into a shallow bowl or tray to allow the custard to cool quickly.

15. Cover the surface with cling film to prevent a skin forming.

16. When cool, whisk until smooth, then add the cream and Armagnac and continue whisking until stiff.

17. Drain and stone the prunes and pipe the custard mixture into each prune.

18. Serve with the shortbread.

Chris Galvin

Pumpkin, Parmesan and
  Chestnut Soup
Roast Sea Bream Au Pistou
Gâteau Basque

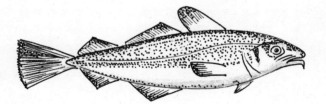

PUMPKIN, PARMESAN AND CHESTNUT SOUP

SERVES 4

1 medium Ironbark pumpkin, skin & seeds removed, flesh cut into large dice
2 medium onions (finely sliced)
125g butter
1 sprig of thyme
1 litre good quality chicken stock
100g Parmesan, finely grated
4 chestnuts, sliced
chopped chives
salt and pepper

METHOD

1. In a large saucepan, gently sweat the finely sliced onions in the butter with the thyme making sure the onions do not colour.

2. When the onions are translucent add the diced pumpkin flesh and season with salt and pepper.

3. Cover the sauce pan with a lid and reduce the heat to allow the pumpkin to soften in its own steam. Check every few minutes to ensure that the pumpkin is not catching on the bottom of the pan.

4. When the pumpkin is tender add the chicken stock and bring to the boil.

5. Add the grated Parmesan.

6. Place the soup in a food processor and blitz until smooth. Check the seasoning

7. Serve in bowls with sliced chestnuts and chopped chives.

ROAST SEA BREAM AU PISTOU

SERVES 4

4 fillets Gilt Head Bream (from a 1kg fish)
150ml extra virgin olive oil
1 finely chopped onion
250g French beans, sliced into 1.5 cm lengths
250g podded fresh small broad beans
100g shelled fresh peas
4 young carrots, sliced
2 courgettes, sliced
100g Charlotte potatoes, diced into 1cm cubes
1.5 litres Vichy mineral water
50g dried noodles, broken into 2cm pieces
2 tomatoes, skinned, seeded and diced
50g Gruyère, finely grated

FOR THE PISTOU:
4 garlic cloves, peeled
8 stems of basil
1 tsp pine nuts
125ml extra virgin olive oil
salt

METHOD

1. First make the pistou. Pound the garlic to a purée in a pestle and mortar, then add the basil leaves and pine nuts and pound with the garlic. Slowly work in the olive oil to form a sauce, then season with salt.

2. For the soup, heat the olive oil in a large pan, add the onion and gently cook until softened. Add the remaining vegetables, cover and sweat gently for a few minutes, without letting them colour. Add the water and bring to the boil. Simmer for about 8 minutes until tender.

CHRIS GALVIN

89

3. Add the noodles and cook for a further 3 minutes. Season to taste.

4. To cook the sea bream, heat 2 non-stick frying pans until very hot, and add 25ml of olive oil to each. Place the sea bream in the pans skin side down, and season with a little salt. Cook for 5 minutes, then turn over and cook for a further 2 minutes.

5. To finish the soup, drop in the tomatoes and pistou, remove from the heat and check the seasoning. Divide between four large, warm soup plates. Sprinkle with the Gruyère, place a bream fillet in each bowl and serve with crusty French baguette.

GÂTEAU BASQUE

SERVES 8

FOR THE PASTRY:
310g plain flour
5g baking powder
4g salt
125g ground almonds
250g butter, diced
2 eggs

FOR THE CUSTARD FILLING:
800ml milk
zest of 2 lemons
zest of 1 orange
1 vanilla pod, split
8 egg yolks
260g sugar
60g plain flour
80g semolina
260ml double cream

2 eggs for glazing the tart
cherry compote, to serve

METHOD

1. First make the pastry by mixing all the dry ingredients in a mixing bowl.

2. Add the diced butter piece by piece and work into the dry ingredients until all the butter is incorporated.

3. Finally add the eggs and work until smooth. Cover with cling film and rest in the fridge.

CHRIS GALVIN

4. When the pastry has rested, remove from the fridge and divide in two.

5. Roll both pieces out to a 5mm thickness.

6. Using a 30cm tart ring, cut a disc out of the pastry and reserve.

7. Use the second portion to line the tart ring, ensuring that you leave a 1cm overlap.

8. Now make the filling for the tart by boiling the milk with the lemon and orange zests and the split vanilla pod.

9. In a large mixing bowl whisk the egg yolks with the sugar, flour and semolina then strain in the boiling milk.

10. Return the mixture to the pan, add the double cream and cook on a low heat until the custard thickens and the semolina has cooked. Remove from the pan and cool.

11. To assemble the tart, fill the lined tart ring to the top with the cold custard mix.

12. Place the disc of pastry on top of the tart and fold the overlapping pastry over the disc to seal the tart.

13. Brush with the two eggs, beaten together, and cook in an oven set at 180°C/Gas mark 4 for 45 minutes.

14. Remove from the oven and cool. Remove the pastry ring and cut the pie into slices. Serve with cherry compote.

Fergus Henderson

Roast Bone Marrow
Smoked Eel, Mash and Bacon
Baked Treacle Pudding

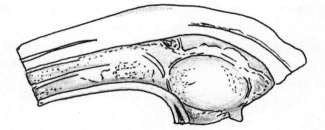

ROAST BONE MARROW

A week before St. John opened, I went to a Saturday afternoon showing of Le Grand Bouffe at the Everyman cinema in Hampstead. The small cinema contained a predictable smattering of foodie pervs. In the film the first meat delivery is celebrated by sucking on roast marrow bones. Here was the dish for me — much to the wife's disappointment: she insisted "they only want chips". On it went, however, and it's never come off the menu in 13 years.

SMOKED EEL, MASH AND BACON

It's amazing how simply delicious things can be.

TREACLE SPONGE

Mum's treacle sponge, things do not get much better. I remember the terrible moment of not being able to eat it and the fear that it had somehow got stuck in my throat. My folks, the hospital and numerous specialists examined the situation. We never knew what gave rise to this, but I'm glad to say my appetite for treacle sponge is back with a vengeance.

ROAST BONE MARROW AND PARSLEY SALAD

SERVES 3–4

12 x 7–8cm pieces of middle veal marrowbone
a healthy bunch of flat-leaf parsley, leaves picked from
the stems
2 shallots, peeled and very thinly sliced
a modest handful of capers (extra-fine if possible)

FOR THE DRESSING:
juice of one lemon
extra virgin olive oil
a pinch of sea salt and pepper

a good supply of toast
coarse sea salt

METHOD

This is the one dish that does not change on the menu at St John.
The marrowbone comes from a calf's leg; ask your butcher to keep
some for you. You will need teaspoons or long thin implements to
scrape the marrow out of the bone.

Do you recall eating Sultana Bran for breakfast? The sultana to
bran-flake ratio was always a huge anxiety, to a point, sometimes,
that one was tempted to add extra sultanas, which inevitably resulted
in too many sultanas, and one lost that pleasure of discovering the
occasional sweet chewiness in contrast to the branny crunch. When
administering such things as capers, it is very good to remember
Sultana Bran.

1. Put the bone marrow in an ovenproof frying pan and place in a
hot oven.

2. The roasting process should take about 20 minutes, depending on
the thickness of the bone. You are looking for the marrow to be loose

FERGUS HENDERSON

95

and yielding, but not melted away, which it will do if left too long (traditionally the ends would be covered to prevent any seepage, but I like the colouring and crispiness at the end).

3. Meanwhile, lightly chop the parsley, just enough to discipline it, mix it with the shallots and capers, and at the last moment, dress.

Here is a dish that should not be completely seasoned before leaving the kitchen, rendering a last minute seasoning necessary by the actual eater; this, especially in the case of the coarse sea salt, gives texture and uplift at the moment of eating. My approach is to scrape the marrow from the bone onto the toast and season with coarse sea salt. Then a pinch of parsley salad on top of this, and eat. Of course, once you have your pile of bones, toast and salt it is 'liberty hall'.

SMOKED EEL, BACON AND MASH

SERVES 3

1 reasonably large whole smoked eel
2kg floury potatoes (Maris Piper are good)
600ml milk
150g unsalted butter
sea salt and pepper
6 thick rashers of good quality smoked streaky bacon

METHOD

More of an assemblage than a recipe as such...

1. To prepare your eel, first lay it down with its back facing you. With a sharp knife cut behind its head until you feel the backbone, then run your knife along the bone to the tail. Turn over and repeat.

2. To remove the skin, simply slip your fingers under it and run gently along the fillet. Cut both fillets into 3 pieces. Smoked eel is also available packaged in fillets.

3. Peel and halve the potatoes and boil them in salted water until soft. Drain well.

4. Heat the milk and butter then add to the drained potatoes and mash. Season to taste, remembering that bacon is quite salty.

5. Heat a frying pan and add a knob of butter. Place the bacon slices in the pan and cook until crisp.

6. When cooked remove the bacon, keep it warm and place the eel fillets in the pan, giving them a few moments cooking either side in the butter and the fat the bacon should have released.

7. Serve the eel on a mound of mashed potato, topped with two slices of bacon, over which pour the remaining bacon- and eel-fat from the frying pan.

FERGUS HENDERSON

97

BAKED TREACLE PUDDING

SERVES 4

100g unsalted butter, softened, plus 2 small knobs of butter
100g caster sugar
2 eggs
100g self-raising flour
Grated zest of 1 lemon
A pinch of sea salt
6 tbsp Golden Syrup (I was advised 4 tbsp by those in the know, but that is simply not enough)

METHOD

The Golden Syrup can be replaced by jam with equally joyous results.

1. To start, take one of your knobs of butter and grease a 500ml pudding basin. For the sponge mixture, cream the butter and sugar with a spoon then add one of the eggs.

2. Mix it in gently with 1 dessertspoon of flour, to prevent the mixture from curdling, then follow with the other egg.

3. Once the eggs, butter and sugar are melded, add the lemon zest and fold in the rest of the flour and salt.

4. Pour the Golden Syrup (or jam) into the pudding basin and then spoon the sponge mixture on top of this.

5. Cover the basin with buttered tin-foil (use knob number two), including a tuck to allow for the expansion of the sponge, then bake in a medium hot oven for 35–40 minutes. It is done when you can stick a skewer in and pull it out clean.

6. When cooked, turn it out onto a warmed dish deep enough for the escaping Golden Syrup (do not worry, this will work). Serve straight away with lots of cream to hand.

Henry Harris

Bayonne Ham and Celeriac
  Remoulade
Georgia's Lamb Stew
Neapolitan Ginger Nut Ice
  Cream Cake

BAYONNE HAM AND CELERIAC REMOULADE

This dish has been on the Racine menu for the last five years. It is such a great starter, savoury and spiky in flavour – I love it.

SERVES 8

4 egg yolks
6 anchovy fillets
3 tbsp Dijon mustard
red wine vinegar
350ml vegetable oil
hot water
salt and pepper
1 large sized head of celeriac or two smaller ones
16 slices Bayonne ham, or its equivalent from Parma or even Serrano
3 tbsp capers

METHOD

1. Place the egg yolks, anchovy fillets, mustard and a splash of red wine vinegar in a food processor. Blitz the mixture to a smooth state and then with the motor running add the oil, initially drop by drop, building up to a more confident stream as the mayonnaise forms. When all the oil is incorporated add a tiny splash of hot water.

2. Check the seasoning, black pepper of course, but perhaps some more mustard may be needed. It should be spiky and assertive.

3. Trim the skin from the celeriac. Now, you need to cut the celeriac into the finest of strips. Use one of two methods. Slice the celeriac as finely as you can and then take those fine slices and cut them into spaghetti-like strips. Alternatively, should you possess one of those lethal, finger shredding Japanese vegetable mandolins, cut the celeriac into manageable chunks, attach the medium strip blade and shred

away using the safety guard to ensure you don't serve your fingers as well.

4. Place the celeriac into a bowl and mix in the mustard mayonnaise. A pair of hands works best.

5. Cover and refrigerate until needed.

6. To serve, place a pile of the celeriac in the middle of each plate. Arrange two slices of ham around the edge of each pile. Sprinkle over a few capers.

GEORGIA'S LAMB STEW

I first cooked a larger version of this recipe for a big gathering to celebrate my daughter Georgia's first birthday. It was the first time as a growing family that we had entertained a large group to celebrate a family occasion. It's not always easy keeping everyone happy and together but feeding them well goes a long way towards helping achieve that goal!

SERVES 8

2kg middle neck fillet of lamb, each cut in half, or shoulder of lamb cut into large dice
salt and pepper
olive oil
4 onions, finely chopped
1 carrot, finely chopped
2 leeks, finely chopped
2 tsp tomato purée
4 garlic cloves, peeled and chopped
2 tins chopped plum tomatoes
4 bay leaves
bottle of red wine
125g good black olives, pitted
1 bunch flat-leaf parsley, leaves picked from stems

FOR THE BEANS:
750g flageolets, soaked overnight in plenty of water
1 carrot
1 onion
1 leek
2 celery sticks
6 garlic cloves, finely chopped
large sprig of rosemary
750ml whipping cream

METHOD

1. Preheat the oven to 180°C/Gas mark 4.

2. Season the lamb fillets with salt and pepper and sauté in a little oil in small batches until well coloured.

3. Transfer to a dish and reserve.

4. Add the onion, carrots, leeks and tomato purée and cook on a low heat for 10 minutes so the vegetables throw off a little liquid. Turn up the heat and continue cooking until the vegetables are lightly browned.

5. Add the garlic and 30 seconds later, the chopped plum tomatoes and bay leaves.

6. Cook on a medium heat for about 20 minutes to reduce the liquid content by half.

7. Add the red wine, bring back to the boil and simmer for 10 minutes.

8. Return the lamb to the pan and place in the oven, uncovered, for about one hour, or until the meat is cooked.

9. Remove the lamb from the oven and gently stir in the black olives. Check the seasoning. This is, as with most stews, much better if done the day before.

10. Strain the beans and place in a large saucepan, cover with plenty of water, bring to the boil and remove the scum. Simmer for 10 minutes and drain. Rinse out the saucepan, return the beans, recover with fresh cold water and bring back to the boil.

11. Lower the heat and simmer for anything from one to two hours. It really does depend on the vintage of your beans. Drain the beans and keep warm.

12. In a separate pan, heat all the other ingredients, season well with

salt and pepper and simmer for 10 minutes. Remove the rosemary, then add this mixture to the beans, stir well and heat through.

13. Place a generous portion of the beans on each plate. Stir the parsley into the lamb and serve with the beans.

NEAPOLITAN GINGER NUT ICE CREAM CAKE

I am not a great pudding lover, a piece of ripe cheese and a glass of red wine will always take first place for me. When it comes to puds it is a case of the simpler the better, or as in this case something that will make the kids smile. No cooking skills are needed here, tubs of premium ice cream will suffice along with some willing smaller hands; there isn't much that can go wrong here.

SERVES 8

200g ginger nut biscuits
125g butter
500ml vanilla ice cream
500ml chocolate ice cream
500ml strawberry ice cream
250g unrefined caster sugar
250g good dark chocolate, broken into pieces

METHOD

1. Take the biscuits and crush them to a coarse powder.

2. Melt the butter and mix it into the crumbs.

3. Spread half the crumb mixture onto the bottom of a 20cm spring-form tin. If the tin isn't non-stick then line the base with greaseproof paper and make a collar to go around the inside edge.

4. Place in the fridge for 30 minutes to firm up.

5. Meanwhile, remove the ice creams from the freezer and let them soften enough to be manageable. The ability of the young cook will be all at this following stage. My preference is to start with a layer of chocolate ice cream. Place all the chocolate ice cream in the base of the pan.

HENRY HARRIS

105

6. Repeat the process with the remaining two ice creams. Then spread on the remaining biscuit mixture.

7. Smooth the top down and place it in the freezer and leave for three hours or more until firm.

8. Take 250ml water and put it in a saucepan along with the sugar. Bring to the boil and when the sugar has dissolved simmer gently for two minutes.

9. Remove from the heat and add the chocolate.

10. Leave for a minute and then whisk gently until smooth.

11. Set aside to cool.

12. Remove the cake from the freezer, undo the spring ring and remove along with the greaseproof paper collar. Cut the cake into wedges and spoon over a little sauce.

Shaun Hill

Cockles and Mussels on Toast
  with Cider Sabayon
Spiced Partridge Pilaf
Chocolate Cake
Chocolate Truffles

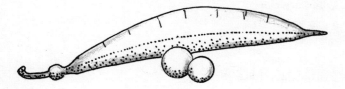

COCKLES AND MUSSELS ON TOAST WITH CIDER SABAYON

The sabayon – zabaione in Italian – is made in a similar way to Hollandaise sauce but is lighter and more fragile because no butter is added.

Points to Watch

The volume of sabayon sauce produced is more dependent on the quantity of cider liquor used than the number of egg yolks used. Try to find a bowl that is as rounded as possible at the base and preferably one that conducts heat easily – stainless steel is ideal but a Pyrex dish would also be okay.

SERVES 4–6

500g mussels
500g cockles
150ml dry cider
3 egg yolks
salt
Tabasco sauce
1 tbsp lemon juice

You will need two saucepans for the dish, one to cook the shellfish, the other to use as a steam bath to whisk sabayon.

METHOD

1. Wash the mussels and tug out any beard that protrudes.

2. Heat the pan and then add both cockles and mussels. Also 100ml of the dry cider.

3. Fit a lid then let the steam evaporating from the cider cook the shellfish – about 3 or 4 minutes only: when the mussels open both they and the cockles will be cooked.

4. Discard the shells then strain the cooking liquor into a bowl —
preferably one without too many corners, more rounded is better —
then whisk the yolks and cider mixture over the hot water. Use a
lifting action as you whisk so that as much air as possible is
incorporated into the sabayon.

5. When the sabayon has risen and thickened it will be ready, needing
only to be seasoned with salt, lemon juice and a few drops of
Tabasco. Reheat the shellfish and make slices of toast.

6. Pile the cockles and mussels onto the hot toast then spoon over
the cider sabayon.

SPICED PARTRIDGE PILAF

The slight gaminess of partridge marries well with soft spices – we are talking coriander and cinnamon here rather than chilli – and so does rice. The stock used to cook the rice will be infused with the same spices and game flavours so that the finished dish seems in harmony rather than just an assembly of disparate ingredients.

SERVES 4

4 partridge
olive oil
1 tsp each cinnamon, cumin, coriander
1 shallot, chopped
1 tbsp chopped celery
250g Basmati rice
1 clove garlic
a little lemon zest
salt and pepper
1 litre (approx) water or chicken stock
15g unsalted butter
1 tbsp chopped fresh coriander leaves
1 tbsp snipped chives

Tips

In spite of anything you may have read, more stock or water can be added to the rice if it is not sufficiently cooked after the initial stock has been absorbed.

To speed the recipe up you can lessen the water or stock, adding say two-thirds of a litre to the rice first of all, then add the partridge's cooking liquor toward the end of the cooking time.

METHOD

1. Separate the legs from the partridges. Fry skin side down and then transfer to a lidded pot with enough water or stock to cover. Braise gently for one hour.

2. Meanwhile, season the remaining crowns of partridge and dust with half the spices. Paint with olive oil or butter and roast in a moderately hot oven – 180°C/Gas mark 4 – until pink. This will take about 25 minutes. When cooked allow to rest for 10 minutes before carving off the breasts.

3. Fry the shallot and celery until they start to colour then add the rice and continue frying for a further 5 minutes. Add salt, pepper and about three time the rice's volume of stock or water. Part of this stock should be made up of the cooking liquor from the partridge legs and the pan residues from the roast partridge crowns.

4. Cook the pilaf on a low heat until most of the liquid has been absorbed then stir in the remaining spices, also the partridge legs and breast to reheat. Finally, stir in a knob of butter and the chopped herbs.

SHAUN HILL

CHOCOLATE CAKE

Chocolate has affinities with many spices, with nuts and with some fruits. Cardamom, cinnamon and vanilla will add a layer of complexity to chocolate mousse or chocolate truffles whilst in no way detracting from the essential chocolate flavour of the prime ingredient. Almonds, walnuts and hazelnuts will act as counterpoint in terms of texture as well as taste — the success of chocolate and nut combinations is witnessed by the amount of commercial choccie bars that rely on this mixture.

Fruit is more controversial and there are plenty that dislike the combination, whatever fruit or grade of chocolate is used. I agree where soft fruits like strawberries and raspberries are concerned but some work well, oranges — especially the peel — bananas, and even passion fruit for instance. Also, cherries which are the classic partner in Black Forest gâteau. This has become a cliché dish, its status not helped by the commercial versions on offer. But as with many other overused and much imitated dishes, the central idea is good. Chocolate, booze soaked cherries and cream make for nice cake.

The chocolate cake below can be partnered by a fresh cherry compote — just bring cherries to the boil with granulated sugar and a few drops of lemon juice — to achieve a decent reworking of the idea in pudding form. Alternatively, you could just make a pot of coffee and eat it as a cake. Cream is optional but the cake will be better for a dollop of crème fraîche, should your dietary regime allow.

SERVES 6–8

225g plain chocolate, broken into pieces
100g unsalted butter
4 eggs, separated into yolks and whites
225g icing sugar
a few drops of vanilla extract
2 tbsp cornflour

Points to watch:

The recipe calls for the chocolate to be melted. This must be done gently and slowly. The chocolate can be grated so that it melts faster if time is important.

There is very little flour — no wheat flour at all — so there may be a tendency for the cake to sag in the middle if not completely cooked through. This is not a huge problem if it happens as there will be no flour to taste raw and uncooked in the finished dish. At worst it will be gooey and fondant. In fact, better undercooked than overcooked.

Vanilla extract or a natural essence from Madagascar are fine. Anything else isn't.

METHOD

1. Melt the chocolate and butter together. The best way to do this is to put the chocolate and butter in a bowl and stand the bowl in warm water, stirring occasionally.

2. Whisk the egg whites until stiff. Make sure to use a clean bowl and whisk.

3. Separately, whisk the yolks, icing sugar and vanilla extract together then add the cornflour. Whisk until the colour of the mixture lightens perceptibly.

4. Add the melted chocolate and butter.

5. Next, add the whisked egg white, folding it in a third at a time.

6. Line an 18cm cake tin with parchment paper and pour in the cake batter.

7. Bake in a hot oven — 190°C/Gas mark 5 — until done, around 30–40 minutes.

CHOCOLATE TRUFFLES

There is a jargon for chocolate work. A mixture of melted chocolate and cream is called ganache. This can be a cake filling but is usually cooled and used mixed with rum or Cointreau to form chocolate truffles. Truffles are the perfect accompaniment to a final coffee in a long meal. They can be flavoured with any spice or liqueur you want and are just fine without any extra flavouring at all.

MAKES 1.5KG

600g couverture chocolate
200ml double cream
300g unsalted butter, softened
50ml rum

TO COAT:
250g couverture, melted
300g cocoa powder

Points to Watch:

Chocolate couverture needs to be melted slowly otherwise it will form white streaks. Leave the grated or chopped chocolate in a bowl over warm water and stir occasionally for the best results.

The boiling of the cream is largely for hygiene and health reasons to sterilise the cream. It keeps better and more safely this way.

The variations on this are endless. Almost any sweet booze or spice can be added as could sultanas soaked in rum or chopped nuts.

METHOD

1. Grate or chop the chocolate and melt gently in a bowl placed over warm water, stirring from time to time.

2. Boil the cream then let it cool.

3. Mix the cream and melted chocolate along with rum or whatever you are using as flavouring.

4. In a large bowl, whisk the softened butter and then pour in the chocolate cream mixture. Refrigerate until ready to use.

5. Make a small production line with the ganache — chocolate mix — the melted couverture and the cocoa powder.

6. Make small balls of ganache with a parisienne cutter or some such — a parisienne cutter is a classic kitchen tool that was used to scoop small balls of potato the size of melon balls to make a fried potato garnish unsurprisingly known as a parisienne potato. Anything similar will do. As would cutting the ganache into whatever shape took your fancy.

7. Use a toothpick to spear each chocolate ball and dip into the melted couverture, then roll in the cocoa powder.

8. Store the truffles in the fridge until needed.

Baba Hine

Wild Garlic and Potato Soup
Pigeon Breasts with
  Mousserons
Three ways with Elderflower

WILD GARLIC AND POTATO SOUP

SERVES 6

500g wild garlic
125g butter
500g diced raw potato
600ml chicken stock
125ml double cream
salt and pepper

METHOD

1. Separate the stalks from the leaves of the wild garlic and reserve the leaves.

2. Take the stalks and sauté them gently in the butter until softened, add the potato and toss in the butter for a few minutes until cooked through, then add the wild garlic leaves and cook until just wilted.

3. Add the chicken stock and bring to the boil.

4. Add the cream, season to taste with salt and pepper.

5. Blitz in a food processor until smooth, put through a sieve and serve with crusty homemade bread.

PIGEON BREASTS WITH MOUSSERONS

SERVES 4

4 pigeons
225g mousseron mushrooms
110g butter
125ml red wine
175ml pigeon stock
salt and pepper

FOR THE STOCK:
1 onion
1 leek
2 sticks celery, diced
2 carrots
bouquet garni

METHOD

1. Slice the pigeon breasts off the bone and skin.

2. Put the carcasses in a large saucepan with the stock vegetables and bouquet garni, fill with water and simmer for six hours. Sieve, cool and refrigerate.

3. Sauté the mousseron mushrooms in the butter with seasoning to taste, remove from the pan and sauté the pigeon breasts in the pan for no more than two minutes. Rremove and keep warm.

4. Deglaze the pan with the red wine and the stock, and reduce to a glossy and syrupy consistency.

5. Divide the mousserons between four plates, slice the pigeon breasts in half and put two on each plate, pour the sauce around and serve.

BABA HINE

119

THREE WAYS WITH ELDERFLOWER – FRITTER, JELLY AND SORBET

SERVES 6

1 bucket of elderflower heads
sugar
1 lemon
6 gelatine leaves
tempura batter
oil for deep frying
icing sugar

FOR THE TEMPURA BATTER:
55g cornflour
115g plain flour
½ teaspoon salt
1 egg
200ml water

METHOD

1. Whisk the tempura ingredients gently together until fairly smooth.

2. Allow to stand for 20 minutes

3. Pick out 12 large heads of elderflower and keep in the fridge. Put the rest of the elderflowers in a large saucepan, cover with water, bring to the boil and then set aside for six hours to infuse. Then pass through a fine sieve. This produces the cordial.

4. To make the sorbet, take a litre of the cordial, add 675g (three cups) of sugar and the juice of the lemon, pour into a sorbetière, churn and freeze.

5. For the jelly, take a further litre of cordial and add sugar to taste, about 350g. Gently heat this mixture until hot and then add the

gelatine leaves and stir to dissolve. Pour into individual moulds and leave to set in the fridge.

6. To serve, dip the heads of elderflower into tempura batter, give them a light shake and deep fry for a minute or two until crisp. Shake icing sugar liberally over, place two on each plate, unmould a jelly onto each plate and add a scoop of sorbet.

Mark Hix

Smoked Salmon with
  Pancakes . . .
Roast Pheasant and
  Chestnuts
Creamed Brussels Sprouts
Christmas Pudding Soufflé

SMOKED SALMON WITH POTATO PANCAKES AND CRÈME FRAÎCHE

This is perfect for brunch or a romantic breakfast, especially if you add a glass or two of buck's fizz. If it seems too much trouble to do first thing in the morning serve it as a starter for dinner. Fishmongers should stock jars of keta (salmon caviare). Beluga or Sevruga caviare can be used if you are feeling a bit flush.

SERVES 4

1 small baking potato, peeled, boiled and mashed
1 small egg
25g plain flour
25g potato flour (optional – replace with ordinary flour if unavailable)
½ tsp baking powder
50ml milk
salt and freshly ground black pepper
a pinch of freshly ground nutmeg
vegetable oil for frying

TO SERVE:
200g good quality smoked salmon, sliced
120g crème fraîche
40–50g salmon caviare (keta)

METHOD

1. Cool the mashed potato then mix in a bowl with the egg, both the flours and the baking powder.

2. Whisk to form a smooth paste by adding the milk a little at a time. Season with salt, pepper and nutmeg.

3. Rub a little oil in a non-stick or your favourite pancake pan, heat gently and pour a quarter of the mixture into the pan. Don't let it

spread too much as the pancakes need to be fairly thick. Turn the pancake over with a spatula after a couple of minutes or when lightly coloured. Then continue with the rest of the mixture, making four pancakes. Leave on a dish ready for serving.

4. When you are ready to eat, warm the pancakes in the oven for about 5 minutes. Arrange the smoked salmon on the pancakes with a spoonful of crème fraîche on top, then spoon the caviare onto the crème fraîche.

ROAST PHEASANT AND CHESTNUTS

Pheasant has a tendency to over-cook and dry out before you know it. By removing the breasts and using the thighs and crumbs to make a stuffing, you end up with a succulent result instead of a completely dry piece of breast and tough old legs. Wrapping them in caul fat helps even more if you can get hold of some as it will stop the juices escaping. If you can't get it from your butcher don't worry.

Serve the pheasants with roasted root vegetables and roast chestnuts, or some seasonal wild mushrooms.

SERVES 4

2 plump pheasants, breasts removed and thighs boned and minced or finely chopped
caul fat, optional

FOR THE STUFFING:
2 shallots, peeled and finely chopped
1 tsp chopped thyme leaves
25g butter, melted
40g fresh white breadcrumbs
meat from the thighs (see above)
1 tbsp chopped parsley
a little vegetable oil
salt and freshly ground black pepper

FOR THE SAUCE:
the bones and drumsticks from the pheasant, chopped
1 onion, peeled and roughly chopped
1 carrot, roughly chopped
a few sprigs of thyme
4 juniper berries
a good knob of butter
½ tbsp flour

50ml red wine
50ml port
1 litre chicken or beef stock
24 lightly roasted and shelled chestnuts or vacuum packed ones

METHOD

1. Preheat the oven to 200°C/Gas mark 6.

2. Roast the bones with the onion and carrot in a roasting tray for about 30 minutes until browned. Remove from the oven and put the tray on a low heat on top of the stove.

3. Add the thyme, juniper berries, butter and flour and stir well.

4. Gradually add the red wine, port and stock, stirring the bottom of the pan well. Bring to the boil, then transfer to a saucepan and simmer gently for about 30 minutes.

5. To make the stuffing, gently cook the shallots and chopped thyme leaves in the butter for 2–3 minutes until soft.

6. Remove from the heat and transfer to a bowl. Add the other ingredients, season with salt and pepper and mix well.

7. Meanwhile, lay the pheasant breasts on a chopping board, skin side down. Remove the fillet and put to one side. With the point of a sharp knife, cut 2 incisions away from the centre of the breast to form a pocket. (Basically, you are just transferring some of the breast meat away from the middle of the breast).

8. Divide the stuffing between the 4 breasts. Flatten the fillet a little with the side of your hand and lay it over the stuffing. Fold the breast meat that you cut previously back into the centre to completely seal in the stuffing.

9. If you are using caul fat, wash it well and wrap each breast a couple times.

10. Heat a roasting tray in the oven with a little oil. Season the pheasant breasts with salt and freshly ground black pepper and cook them in the oven for 5–6 minutes, turning once.

11. Meanwhile, strain the sauce through a fine-mesh sieve and simmer it on a medium heat until it thickens.

12. Add the chestnuts and warm them through. If the sauce is not thick enough, dilute a little cornflour with water, stir it into the sauce and simmer for a couple of minutes.

13. Serve the breasts cut in half with the sauce poured over.

CREAMED BRUSSELS SPROUTS

A simple way to use up left over sprouts or prepare them from fresh and serve with game dishes.

SERVES 4–6

1kg large Brussels sprouts, prepared and cooked
200ml double cream
salt and freshly ground black pepper
60g butter

METHOD

1. Slice the sprouts thinly.

2. Reduce the cream by half then add the sprouts and season with salt and pepper.

3. Simmer for 4–5 minutes on a low heat, stirring every so often.

4. Add the butter and serve.

CHRISTMAS PUDDING SOUFFLÉ

SERVES 8

FOR THE FILLING:
50g double cream
70g dark chocolate, chopped
20ml Drambuie
50g mincemeat

METHOD

1. Bring the cream to the boil, remove from the heat and stir in the chocolate until melted.

2. Stir in the Drambuie and mincemeat and leave to cool.

3. When cool, mould into rough even-sized balls.

FOR THE SOUFFLÉ:
1 ready-made sponge cake
300g butter
300g white chocolate
10g baking powder
¼ tsp mixed spice
¼ tsp ground cinnamon
240g flour
5 eggs, separated
90g caster sugar
30g dried mixed fruits, soaked in hot water

butter and caster sugar, for dusting the rings

METHOD

1. Lightly butter and dust with caster sugar the inside of eight 8cm stainless steel rings, or deep egg poaching rings. Cut eight discs of

sponge 8cm wide and ½ cm thick and place them inside the rings on a buttered baking sheet, 6–7 cm apart.

2. Preheat the oven to 190°C/Gas mark 5.

3. Melt the butter and white chocolate in a bowl over a pan of simmering water.

4. Meanwhile, sift together the baking powder, spices and flour.

5. Mix the egg yolks into the chocolate, then gently fold in the sieved flour mixture.

6. Whisk the egg whites and sugar until stiff and then fold into the mix.

7. Half fill the moulds then add a ball of the filling and top up with the rest of the mixture.

8. Bake the soufflés for 10–12 minutes, remove from the oven, loosen with a knife and carefully put onto warmed serving plates with a spatula. Serve with pouring cream or as they are, as the filling acts as a sauce.

Ken Hom

Red Cooked Chicken Wings
Steamed Salmon with Black
 Bean Sauce
Papaya and Grapefruit Salad

I love these recipes because it means I can entertain with a casual nonchalance and have fun with my guests. These are easy recipes that guarantee success every time, no matter the size of the crowd you will be cooking for!

RED COOKED CHICKEN WINGS

"Red cooking" simply means simmering in a richly flavoured sauce that also imparts a deep red colour to the food. Here, I use chicken wings, the tastiest and most underrated part of the chicken, and the result is a tempting dish, nicely re-heatable and rather quick to make. Just about 30 minutes to create a most satisfying and unusual starter.

SERVES 4–6

750g chicken wings
1 tbsp oil, preferably groundnut
1 tbsp coarsely chopped fresh ginger
½ tsp salt
2 tbsp dark soy sauce
1 tbsp rice wine or dry sherry
3 tbsp hoisin sauce
2 tsp sugar
2 tsp chilli bean sauce
150ml water

METHOD

1. Cut the wings in half at the joint.

2. Heat a wok or large frying pan until it is hot, then add the oil, ginger and salt. Stir-fry the mixture for 10 seconds.

3. Add the rest of the ingredients and simmer for 1 minute.

4. Put in the wings, cover the wok, and cook for 15 minutes, or until the wings are cooked through.

5. Serve at once or let cool and serve at room temperature.

Hint:

You can make this also with chicken thighs and legs.

The recipe can easily be doubled for a larger crowd.

STEAMED SALMON WITH BLACK BEAN SAUCE

Fresh salmon is a luxury which everyone can now enjoy. Prepare it using this Chinese steaming method: it preserves all the noble richness of the salmon. Here, I use a traditional black bean sauce. It has a very pleasantly pungent taste that actually enhances the distinctive salmon flavour, making a wonderful contrast on the palate. This simple dish would grace a dinner party as a main course.

SERVES 4–6

450g fresh boneless salmon fillets, sliced 2.5cm thick
1 tsp salt
2 tsp sesame oil
1 tbsp oil, preferably groundnut
2 tbsp black beans, coarsely chopped
1½ tbsp coarsely chopped garlic
1 tbsp finely chopped fresh ginger
3 tbsp coarsely chopped spring onions
1 tbsp dark soy sauce
2 tsp light soy sauce
150ml water

METHOD

1. Set a rack into a wok or deep pan. Fill with 6cm water and bring to a simmer.

2. Rub the salmon fillets with the salt and sesame oil and place on a heatproof plate. Place the plate with the salmon on top of the rack, cover tightly and steam for 6 minutes.

3. While the salmon is steaming, heat a wok or large frying pan until it is hot, then add the oil, black beans, garlic and ginger. Stir-fry the mixture for 1 minute, then add the spring onions, soy sauces and water and simmer for 1 minute.

4. When the salmon is cooked, pour the hot sauce over the salmon and serve at once.

Hint:

It is best to undercook the salmon slightly as it continues to cook even after it has been removed from the steamer.

Substitute other fresh fish fillets such as haddock or cod.

For another variation, you can use fresh scallops.

PAPAYA AND GRAPEFRUIT SALAD

Grapefruit are sometimes taken for granted, their tartness and sweetness overlooked in this age of more glamorous fare. But they take on an extra dimension with the papaya (pawpaw) companion and the result is a refreshing dessert after the spiciness of the starter and main course. For more colour and elegance, add fresh strawberries or raspberries.

SERVES 4

1 papaya fruit
2 grapefruit
2 tbsp lemon juice
2 tbsp sugar

METHOD

1. Slice the papaya in half lengthways and remove the seeds.

2. Peel away the outside skin and cut the papaya into slices. Peel and slice the grapefruit into segments. Arrange the fruits on a platter and sprinkle with the lemon juice and sugar.

3. Wrap the bowl tightly in clingfilm until you are ready to serve.

Simon Hopkinson

Chilled and Jellied Beetroot
  Consommé
Chicken Sautéed with Red
  Wine Vinegar
Saint-Emilion au Chocolat

CHILLED AND JELLIED BEETROOT CONSOMMÉ

This is a glorious cold soup. Its very colour is quite magnificent and it should always be served in pristine white soup plates for the most dramatic effect. For the liquid, beef broth is the traditional Russian flavour and duck stock can be particularly fine too: the perfect use for a left over carcass from a roast. If you want a beefy flavour, ask your butcher to cut you a large slice off a shin of beef, bone included, and then seal it all over in the vegetable oil until a deep brown colour is achieved, before adding the vegetables and liquid. Incidentally, I have made a very passable chilled borscht using canned beef consommé. You might think that this whole recipe is a palaver. You might well be right. But wait until you taste the result.

SERVES 6

2 tbsp vegetable oil

500g chicken wings, chopped up a bit

1 large carrot, peeled and chopped

2 sticks celery, chopped

2 leeks, cleaned and sliced

2 cloves garlic, bashed

a little salt

a few black peppercorns

1 peeled onion, stuck with 3 cloves

2 sprigs fresh thyme

2 bay leaves

2.5 litres water

4 fresh, raw beetroot, peeled and grated

2 wine glasses ruby port

2 beaten egg whites

110g lean minced beef

3 cooked beetroot

1 tbsp red wine vinegar

150ml sour cream, thinned with a little milk
paprika
snipped chives

METHOD

1. In the base of a large, heavy bottomed stew-pan, heat the oil until smoking.

2. Put in the wings and fry for a couple of minutes until lightly browned.

3. Tip the pan a little and spoon out any excess fat.

4. Put in all the vegetables, seasoning and herbs.

5. Fill with water and bring to the boil. Skim off any surface scum and put to simmer for 1½ hours on a very low heat, or even in the oven (140°C/Gas mark 1), uncovered.

6. Strain through a roomy colander and allow to drip for 10 minutes or so, then pass the broth through a damp, folded sheet of muslin into a large clean stainless steel or enamelled pan.

7. Remove any fat from the surface with several sheets of kitchen paper. Then simmer the stock and reduce gently, skimming the surface of any scum that forms during the process.

8. When the stock measures about 1 litre (this does not have to be dead accurate), remove from the heat and leave to cool until lukewarm.

9. In a roomy bowl, with your hands, mulch together the raw beetroot, port, egg whites and minced beef. Tip into the stock and whisk together.

10. Put back onto a moderate heat and return to the merest simmer.

11. During this stage, make sure that the mulched mixture does not stick to the bottom of the pan; feel around with a wooden spoon

perhaps, but do not disturb the beetroot/mince crust that forms on the surface.

12. Simmer gently for 40 minutes. What is happening now is a clarification process; the egg whites and natural albumen in the meat are collecting all the impurities in the stock into themselves, whilst the meat, grated beetroot and port are also flavouring the stock. As the stock gently blips through the crust it should be clear and ruby red. After the 40 minutes is up, make a hole in the crust with a spoon and lift some of it away. Now using a ladle, transfer the clear liquid that lies beneath, through a muslin-lined sieve into a clean pan. Collect all you can. Discard the crust, it has done its work.

13. Now grate the cooked beetroot into the hot, clear beetroot-flavoured stock (consommé) together with the vinegar and gently stir together. Cover and leave to infuse for 1 hour.

14. Drain for the last time, just through a fine sieve, into a clean bowl.

15. Use the sieved/cooked beetroot in a salad for another time.

16. Put the beetroot consommé into the fridge and allow to set to a jellied consistency.

17. When cold and jellied, spoon out into chilled soup plates and decorate with a slurry of sour cream, a shake of paprika and some chives.

18. Serve with buttered rye bread and a glass of iced vodka.

CHICKEN SAUTÉED WITH RED WINE VINEGAR

This very simple dish is a great favourite. Its success lies in the fact that there are very few ingredients other than a good chicken and excellent quality vinegar.

SERVES 4

1.8kg chicken, jointed into 8 pieces
salt and pepper
110g butter
2 tbsp olive oil
6 very ripe tomatoes, skinned, seeded and chopped
300ml best quality red wine vinegar
300ml chicken stock
2 heaped tbsp chopped parsley

METHOD

1. Season the joints of chicken with salt and pepper.

2. Heat 50g of the butter and the olive oil in a flameproof casserole until just turning nut brown.

3. Add the chicken and fry gently, turning occasionally, until golden brown all over.

4. Add the chopped tomatoes, and carry on frying until the tomato has lost its moisture and is dark, red and sticky.

5. Pour in the vinegar and reduce by simmering until almost disappeared. Add the stock and simmer again until reduced by half.

6. Remove the chicken to a serving dish and keep warm.

7. Whisk the remaining butter into the sauce to give it a glossy finish.

8. Add 1 tbsp chopped parsley, pour over the chicken and sprinkle with the remaining parsley.

9. Serve with plain boiled potatoes.

SIMON HOPKINSON

SAINT-EMILION AU CHOCOLAT

I think it must have been during the 1960's that this wonderfully rich chocolate dessert started appearing on menus. I am sure I am right in saying that George Perry-Smith, from the famous Hole in the Wall restaurant in Bath, was the initiator, although the original recipe comes from Elizabeth David's French Country Cooking.

SERVES 4

110g unsalted butter, softened
110g caster sugar
1 egg yolk
200ml milk
225g dark, bitter chocolate, broken into pieces
12–16 macaroons or Italian amaretti biscuits
a little rum or brandy

METHOD

1. Cream the butter and sugar together until light and fluffy.

2. Beat in the egg yolk.

3. Heat the milk and chocolate, stirring occasionally, until melted and smooth.

4. Allow to cool slightly then add to the butter/sugar mixture and beat well.

5. Arrange some of the macaroons in a soufflé dish or four individual ramekins, using just enough to cover the base. Sprinkle over some of the rum or brandy.

6. Cover with a layer of the chocolate mixture, add a further layer of biscuits, a little more rum or brandy and another layer of chocolate.

7. Depending on the size of your dish or dishes, carry on in this fashion until both biscuits and chocolate are used up.

8. Chill for at least 12 hours or overnight before serving.

Nigel Howarth

Forager's Soup
Goats Cheese Gnocchi
Lancashire Hot Pot
Pickled Red Cabbage
Barber Green Pudding with
  Raspberries

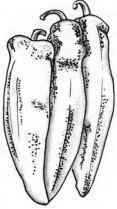

FORAGER'S SOUP (BITTERCRESS, NETTLE, CHERVIL AND WILD GARLIC) WITH GOATS CHEESE GNOCCHI

SERVES 4

200g foraged leaves, washed thoroughly
100g finely sliced onions
150g thinly sliced potato
1–2 cloves garlic, finely chopped
100g butter
100ml cream
1 litre hot chicken stock

METHOD

1. Sweat the onions in the butter in a heavy bottom pan, add the potatoes and garlic and sweat for a further minute. (To sweat is to cook without colour in a covered pan, on a moderate to hot temperature).

2. Add the hot chicken stock and cream, and cook until the potatoes are soft (approx 5–10 minutes).

3. Add the greens and bring back to the boil. Liquidise slowly, then pass through a fine sieve into a clean bowl. Cool down quickly over ice and reserve.

4. Reheat the soup at the same time as pan-frying the gnocchi (see below). Divide the soup between warmed bowls, add some gnocchi to each bowl and serve hot.

GOATS CHEESE GNOCCHI

SERVES 4–6

350g Desirée potatoes
1 egg
150g pasta flour
100g grated goats cheese

METHOD

1. Bake the whole potatoes in the oven.

2. When cooked, scrape the potato out of the skin and put through a potato ricer into a mixing bowl. Mix all the ingredients together gently until combined.

3. Roll into a long cylinder and cut into 3cm long pieces.

4. With a fork, gently pull forwards on the gnocchi to make grooves.

5. Blanch in salted boiling water, refresh in ice water and reserve.

6. When ready to serve, heat some olive oil until hot and pan fry the gnocchi until golden.

NIGEL HOWARTH

LANCASHIRE HOT POT

In the heart of Lancashire, I would always use heather-fed Bowland Lamb. Hotpot can be made anywhere and I would always use the local lamb from the region.

SERVES 4

1kg shoulder, neck and shin of lamb (cut into 3-4cm thick pieces)
700g thinly sliced onions
700g peeled King Edward potatoes
25g plain flour
40g salted butter, melted
150ml chicken stock
3 tsp sea salt
white pepper

METHOD

1. Season the lamb with a teaspoon of salt and a good pinch of pepper, and dust with the flour. Put the lamb into the base of a 20cm wide, 9cm high hot pot dish.

2. Sweat the onions in 15g butter with 1 teaspoon salt for 4–5 minutes (to sweat is to cook without colour in a covered pan, on a moderate to hot temperature). Spread the onions evenly on top of the lamb in the hot pot dish.

3. Slice the potatoes horizontally to a thickness of 2mm. Place in a medium size bowl, add the remaining 25g melted butter, season with 1 teaspoon of salt and a pinch of white pepper and mix well.

4. Put the sliced potatoes evenly on top of the onions, reserving the best shaped rounds for the final layer.

5. Place the hotpot, covered, in a pre-heated oven set to 180–200°C/Gas mark 4–6 (Aga equivalent bottom of the baking oven) for 30 minutes then reduce the temperature to 130°C/Gas mark 1 (Aga equivalent is the simmering oven) for a further 2½ hours.

6. Remove from the oven, take off the lid or cover, return to the oven set back to 180–200°C/Gas mark 4–6 (Aga equivalent bottom of the roasting oven) for 30–40 minutes or until golden brown.

7. Serve with pickled red cabbage.

NIGEL HOWARTH

PICKLED RED CABBAGE

This can be made a day in advance

SERVES 4–6

1 head of red cabbage
coarse sea salt for salting the cabbage
275ml malt vinegar
140ml white wine vinegar
140ml balsamic vinegar
400ml red wine
12oz caster sugar
2 star anise
5 bay leaves
10 whole cloves
1 tsp whole black peppercorns
1 tsp whole pink peppercorns
1 stick cinnamon, snapped in half
5 whole dried red chillies

METHOD

1. Quarter the red cabbage.

2. De-vein the large stem and finely slice the red cabbage leaves. (Alternatively, put through a food processor)

3. Salt the red cabbage well and leave in a colander for 2–3 hours until a deep rich colour is achieved.

4. Drain and wash all the salt away thoroughly, then pat dry.

5. Place all the vinegars, wine and sugar in a suitable pan and reduce by half.

6. Place all the dry ingredients in a pestle and mortar and pound to a coarse consistency.

7. When the reduction is near completion, throw the dry spice mixture into the reduction and allow to infuse for 5 minutes. Pass the reduction through a fine sieve and while still warm pour onto the red cabbage.

8. Place the cabbage in a suitable jar and seal. The liquor should just cover the cabbage.

BARBER GREEN PUDDING WITH RASPBERRIES

SERVES 4

600ml milk
zest of 1 lemon
50g unsalted butter
50g caster sugar
100g fresh white breadcrumbs
6 egg yolks
4 dssp raspberry jam

FOR THE MERINGUE:
4 egg whites
220g caster sugar

fresh raspberries to serve

METHOD

1. In a heavy bottom pan, bring the milk and lemon to the boil, add the butter and caster sugar, and mix well. Stir in the bread crumbs and allow to cool slightly.

2. Whisk in the egg yolks thoroughly.

3. Divide equally between four large ramekin dishes (approx 11cm x 4cm).

4. Place the ramekins in a bain-marie (deep tray lined with paper then filled with hot water to a depth of approx 2cm). Bake in the oven at 140°C/Gas mark 2 for 15–20 minutes until the puddings are set.

5. Remove the puddings from the oven and allow to cool, then spoon on the raspberry jam.

6. Beat the egg whites with a little of the sugar until they form stiff peaks, then gradually fold in the rest of the sugar.

7. Pipe the meringue on top of the jam to form small peaks, totally covering the top of each pudding.

8. Bake for a further 5 minutes at 200°C/Gas mark 6

9. Serve with fresh cream and raspberries.

Tom Kitchin

Scallops, Pancetta and
 Asparagus
Roast Loin of Lamb ...
Peppered Parfait ...

SCALLOPS, PANCETTA AND ASPARAGUS

At the restaurant these are West Coast hand-dived scallops with
roast Spring asparagus from Glamis in Perthshire, served with a herb
beurre blanc.

SERVES 1

2 slices of finely sliced pancetta
2 cocktail sticks
2 hand-dived scallops
4 spears of asparagus
olive oil
sea salt

FOR THE SAUCE:
100ml white wine
1 shallot, thinly sliced
10 cracked peppercorns
1 spoonful of cream
150g non-salted butter
sherry vinegar
chervil and dill for garnish

METHOD

1. Wrap the pancetta around the middle of the scallops (ensuring the
pancetta goes all the away round).

2. Insert a cocktail stick to hold the pancetta securely in place
during cooking.

3. Prepare the asparagus by removing the woody ends.

4. Place the asparagus in a hot frying pan with olive oil and salt and
cook until tender.

5. In another pan, sear the pancetta-wrapped scallops The pancetta will give great flavour to the scallops.

6. To make the sauce, place the white wine in a pan, add the sliced shallot and the cracked peppercorns and reduce until almost dry.

7. Add a spoonful of cream to stabilise the sauce, then whisk in the butter.

8. Season with salt and maybe a dash of sherry vinegar if needed.

9. Pass it through a sieve.

10. Place the roast asparagus on a plate.

11. Place the roast scallops on top.

12. Drizzle the sauce around the asparagus and scallops.

13. Garnish with sprigs of chervil and dill.

ROAST LOIN OF LAMB WITH COMPOTE OF RED ONION, SZECHWAN PEPPER AND LEMON.

SERVES 4

1 loin of lamb
olive oil
2 red onions, sliced
1 tsp Szechwan pepper wrapped in a muslin cloth
½ tsp coriander seeds
zest and juice of half a lemon
300ml lamb jus
50g dried apricots, finely chopped
salt and pepper

METHOD

1. Sweat the onions slowly in a little olive oil for 10 minutes with Szechwan pepper, coriander seeds and lemon zest.

2. Add lemon juice and lamb jus along with the dried apricots and a little salt and cook gently for 45 minutes until onions and jus form a compote.

3. Brush the loin of lamb with olive oil, season lightly and roast in a hot oven until pink in the centre.

4. Carve and serve on top of the compote, accompanied by French beans and seasonal vegetables.

PEPPERED PARFAIT OF ICED PERTHSHIRE HEATHER HILLS HONEY WITH KUMQUAT MARMALADE.

SERVES 4

FOR THE PARFAIT:
90g honey
4 egg yolks
300ml whipping cream
1½ tsp cracked black pepper

FOR THE KUMQUAT MARMALADE:
400g kumquats, washed and halved
100g dried apricots, thinly sliced
350g sugar

METHOD

1. Bring the honey to the boil in a small saucepan.

2. Place the egg yolks in a mixer bowl fitted with a whisk and start the motor. Slowly add the hot honey to the yolks while whisking, and continue whisking until light and creamy.

3. Separately whip the cream to soft peaks, then fold the pepper into the cream.

4. Fold the honey mousse into the peppered cream.

5. Pour into moulds and freeze.

6. Place the kumquats and apricots in a non-reactive saucepan and cover with water.

7. Bring to a boil and simmer for 20 minutes.

8. Strain and set the fruit aside. Return 300ml of the cooking liquid to the pan and add the sugar.

9. Bring to the boil and allow to bubble for 10–15 minutes before adding the fruit to the pan.

10. Reduce gently until thick.

11. Cool and refrigerate, covered, until ready to serve.

12. Unmould the honey parfaits and serve each with a little of the marmalade.

Jeremy Lee

Beetroot Salad
Loin of Venison, Prunes and
  Mashed Potato
Gâteau St. Victoire

BEETROOT SALAD

SERVES 6–8

2kg smaller-sized beetroots of every colour and variety

125g caster sugar

250ml very good red wine vinegar

150ml water

6 eggs

2 tbsp caster sugar

2 tbsp white wine vinegar

2 tbsp good Dijon mustard

6 tbsp double cream

a stick of horseradish

salad leaves

chopped chives (optional)

salt and pepper

METHOD

1. Trim and wash well the beetroots and place in a suitable pot to steam until quite cooked through and tender.

2. When done, remove the beetroots to a bowl and once cooled slightly rub the skins away. When all are peeled, cut the beetroots into large pieces, random shapes of roughly the same size.

3. In a bowl whisk the sugar with the vinegar until it is dissolved and add the water. Pour this light pickle over the beetroots and cover well. Refrigerate. These pickles will happily last a week in the fridge.

4. Bring a pan of water to a furious boil. Drop in the eggs and let cook for 3 minutes once the water has returned to the boil. Remove the eggs to a bowl of iced water and once cooled peel carefully, storing them in another bowl of iced water.

5. To make the dressing dissolve the sugar and the vinegar in a bowl.

Stir in the mustard until smooth and then add the cream. Pour into a bowl, cover and refrigerate.

6. Peel the horseradish and keep covered until needed.

7. Wash the salad leaves, dry well and keep covered.

8. Should chives be at hand then slice them very thinly in readiness.

9. Tumble the salad leaves onto a plate, then heap the beetroots thereon. Cut the egg in half and lay upon the beetroots, seasoning with a little salt and pepper. Liberally spoon over the mustard dressing and then grate horseradish all over swiftly, followed by the chives.

LOIN OF VENISON, PRUNES & MASHED POTATO

This is the type of dish the British excel at. Handsome, impressive and in preparation quite simple, provided the butcher has been politely asked to trim the meat and tie it up rather neatly. The venison should be cooked to a degree that leaves it pink in the middle, as it is a lean meat and can be dry, which is a very good reason to serve up a bowl of prunes simmered in wine and blackcurrant jelly. This excellent accompaniment benefits from sitting for several days beforehand. Served up with a creamy mash and a great bunch of green watercress, the dish looks as delicious as it tastes.

SERVES 6, ALTHOUGH THE TRENCHERMAN MAY WISH TO ADD MORE TO THE POT

An impressive loin of venison weighing 1–1.2kg, trimmed and tied by a butcher
3 tbsp olive oil
sea salt
a fully charged pepper mill

FOR THE PRUNES:
70ml red wine
4 tbsp blackcurrant jelly
24 large plump prunes, the stones remaining within
a clove
a shard of cinnamon stick
4 black peppercorns, cracked

TO SERVE:
a great pot of creamy, buttery mashed potatoes
a big bunch of watercress

METHOD

1. Warm the oven to 200°C/Gas mark 6.

2. Next cook the prunes. In a heavy bottomed pot, warm the wine and the blackcurrant jelly. When dissolved add the prunes, the clove, cinnamon stick and peppercorns. Stir in the prunes and mix well.

3. Simmer the prunes for a few minutes, then remove from the heat. Place in a ceramic bowl and cover. Keep in a cool place until required to serve with the venison.

4. Liberally anoint the loin with the olive oil and generously season with salt and pepper. Warm a heavy pan and lay in the loin of venison.

5. Let sit undisturbed, having a care that the meat does not get too hot and scorch. Turn after 7 or 8 minutes, the meat dark and crusted, and repeat thus until done all over. Pop in the oven for 5–8 minutes only, until the meat is resilient to a prod. Remove from the oven and let the venison rest in the pot a while. Do this at least 10 minutes before slicing.

6. Have the mash ready and the watercress prepared. The prunes can be warmed or served at room temperature. Slice the meat and anoint with a dab of juice from the pot. Serve up with the mash and watercress with prunes to the side.

GÂTEAU ST. VICTOIRE

SERVES 6–8

350g best bitter dark chocolate
3 tbsp espresso coffee
9 eggs
175g caster sugar
425ml double cream
3 tbsp rum
1 tsp vanilla extract
75g cocoa powder

METHOD

1. Heat the oven to 150°C/Gas mark 3.

2. Line a sealed cake tin with silicon paper.

3. Have ready a bain-marie large enough to accommodate the cake tin.

4. Melt the chocolate gently along with the espresso.

5. Whisk the eggs and sugar until pale and voluminous.

6. Whisk the cream into soft peaks.

7. Fold the cream into the egg mixture, then add the chocolate, rum, vanilla extract and cocoa.

8. Tip the cake mix into the tin and place in the bain-marie. Bake for 25–30 minutes and let sit for a wee bit before serving.

9. Loves a dod of whipped cream.

Rowley Leigh

Spaghetti with Sardines,
  Rocket and Anchovy Crumbs
Spiced Chicken with Button
  Onions and Raisins
Semolina Pudding with Blood
  Oranges and Rhubarb

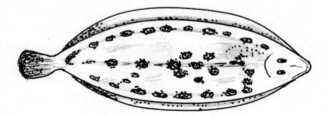

SPAGHETTI WITH SARDINES, ROCKET AND ANCHOVY CRUMBS

In the spring, young nettle leaves can be substituted for the rocket – they lose their sting as soon as they are heated through.

SERVES 4

10 anchovy fillets
50ml virgin olive oil
6 tbsp fresh breadcrumbs
400g spaghetti
100g tinned sardines
2 cloves garlic
1 tbsp virgin olive oil
A large pinch of chilli flakes
finely grated zest of 1 lemon
50g rocket
salt

METHOD

1. Chop the anchovy fillets very finely before heating the oil in a frying pan. Add the anchovies and simmer them in the oil for a minute or two until they disintegrate before adding the breadcrumbs.

2. Turn up the heat and stir the breadcrumbs steadily until they fry to a lovely golden brown. Pour them into a sieve, discarding the oil.

3. Put a large pot of water on to boil with a handful of salt. Drop the spaghetti into the boiling water. Separate the strands of spaghetti with a fork and allow to cook at a good boil.

4. Drain and break up the sardines into small pieces, retaining the oil from the tin. Peel the garlic, chop it finely and stew it gently in a tablespoon of olive oil in a second large saucepan. Add the chilli flakes and the sardines and heat through.

5. As soon as the spaghetti has cooked, drain it and add to the pan with the sardines.

6. Moisten with a little of the cooking water and add the lemon zest and rocket. Turn this mixture well on the heat, adding a little of the oil from the sardine tin if the spaghetti needs lubrication. Check the seasoning and serve, sprinkling the anchovy crumbs on top.

SPICED CHICKEN WITH BUTTON ONIONS AND RAISINS

Necessity being the mother of invention, this is the result of finding nothing in the fridge apart from a lovely chicken, a small bag of pickling onions wandering towards their sell by date and a very healthy cos lettuce. The rest came from the store cupboard. It worked very well.

SERVES 4

1 chicken, around 1.8kg
4 cloves garlic
1 tsp sea salt
1 tsp black peppercorns
the heads of 6 cloves
the seeds from 4 cardamom pods
1 dessertspoon fennel seeds
a pinch of saffron
2 pinches crushed chilli flakes
juice of 1 lemon
3 tbsp virgin olive oil
500g button onions
2 tbsp raisins
25g butter
1 tbsp light brown caster sugar
1 tsp ground cinnamon
3 tbsp red wine vinegar
400g peeled chopped tomatoes
150ml white wine (optional)

METHOD

1. Cut the chicken into 8 pieces (the legs cut in half, the wings with a piece of the breast attached and the breast pieces themselves).

2. Pound the garlic and sea salt with a mortar and pestle to a paste.

3. In a dry frying pan roast the peppercorns, cloves, cardamom and fennel seeds over a high flame until they start to brown and give off a strong aroma. Transfer these spices to the mortar and continue to pound them with the garlic and salt until you achieve a smooth paste.

4. Add the saffron, the chilli flakes, lemon juice and a tablespoon of olive oil and work into a paste again. Rub this paste into the chicken pieces thoroughly and leave to marinade for at least an hour and up to 24 hours.

5. Soak the onions in warm water for 20 minutes before peeling them, taking care to cut them right at the base so that they remain intact when cooked.

6. Pour some boiling water over the raisins and let them also soak for at least 20 minutes.

7. Heat a little olive oil and the butter in a frying pan and add the peeled onions. Colour the onions, shaking them from time to time, for 3 to 4 minutes before sprinkling over the sugar and the cinnamon and continuing cooking until they start to caramelise.

8. Add the vinegar and reduce this violently until there is a scant tablespoon. Add the chopped tomatoes and a small cup of water, turn the heat down low and simmer gently for 20 minutes or until the onions are tender. Add the raisins and leave to cool.

9. Meanwhile, heat a large frying pan with the remaining 2 tablespoons of olive oil and proceed to fry the chicken pieces, skin side down at first, on a gentle heat so that they slowly colour on every side.

10. Pour out any oil and fat from the pan and pour in the wine (water will do). Scrape up any residue from the pan and add the onion and tomato mixture and simmer gently for 20 minutes, removing the breast pieces as soon as they are cooked through. This dish can be served straightaway or reheated at leisure, and needs only some fluffy white rice and a sharp green salad by way of accompaniment.

SEMOLINA PUDDING WITH BLOOD ORANGES AND RHUBARB

The rhubarb and orange compote can accompany a good many things – a pannacotta springs to mind – but I am a sucker for a good milk pudding.

SERVES 8

1 litre milk
2 vanilla pods
250g semolina
5 blood oranges
125g butter
300g light brown caster sugar
5 eggs, separated
2 extra egg whites
6 long stalks early forced rhubarb
extra butter for ramekins

METHOD

1. Pour the cold milk into a saucepan and add 1 of the vanilla pods, having split it down the middle and scraped some of the seeds into the milk. Bring this gently to the boil before adding the semolina in a thin stream, whisking it well.

2. Continue to cook this mixture, stirring it very regularly, until the semolina is cooked and has thickened the milk, which will take about 10 minutes.

3. Add the finely grated zest of 2 of the blood oranges and the butter and whisk well.

4. In a separate bowl whisk together a third (100g) of the sugar and the egg yolks. Slowly pour the semolina into the egg yolk mixture, whisking constantly, and allow to cool.

5. Whisk all 7 egg whites with another third of the sugar in an electric mixer until they form stiff peaks. Fold a third of the whites into the cool (not cold) semolina mixture and mix well before folding in the remainder.

6. Butter very well eight 125g or 150g ramekin moulds (or similar). Pour the semolina mixture into the ramekins and place them in a deep ovenproof tray. Pour boiling water into the tray just over half way up the ramekins and cover loosely with foil.

7. Place in a preheated oven (180°C/Gas mark 4) and bake for 45 minutes or until the centres of the puddings are firm to the touch. Remove the ramekins to a wire rack and allow to cool.

8. Bring ½ litre of water to the boil with the remaining 100g of sugar and the second vanilla pod, again split in half and the seeds scraped into the water. Once the sugar is dissolved take off the heat and leave to infuse for 10 minutes.

9. Wash the rhubarb then cut the stalks into 3cm lengths. Bring the syrup back to the boil, add the rhubarb, cover and remove from the heat. The rhubarb should be just tender when the syrup has cooled.

10. Cut off the tops and bottoms of the oranges. Peel away the skin with a small sharp knife as though removing the staves of a barrel, making sure there is no white pith left on the fruit. Remove the segments of fruit with the knife from between the walls of skin and collect them and their juice in a bowl.

11. Combine the orange segments with the rhubarb once it has cooled.

12. Once cool, run a little knife around the inside of the ramekins and gently invert the semolina puddings onto individual plates. Spoon the rhubarb and orange mixture around.

Bruce Poole

Leek and Potato Soup ...
Slow Roast Shoulder of
  Lamb ...
Vanilla Custard with
  Raspberries

LEEK AND POTATO SOUP WITH SAFFRON, SMOKED HADDOCK, POACHED EGG AND CHIVES

SERVES 4

3 big leeks
1 big knob of butter (about 75g) plus extra for croutons
1 peeled big floury potato (Maris Piper or Desirée is fine)
pinch of saffron threads
850ml light chicken stock
a thick slice of bread, preferably sourdough
a little double cream or crème fraîche
1 large skinned and boned fillet of smoked haddock
4 fresh eggs
1 bunch of chives
salt and pepper

METHOD

1. Wash the leeks and cut them into even 1cm dice then sweat in the butter in a big, deep pan.

2. Peel the spud again, and chop into even 1cm dice.

3. When the leek has softened in the butter add the potato and the saffron threads. Season well and cover with the chicken stock. Bring to a simmer and skim. Do not over-skim or you will remove all the butter, which is a shame as it adds a pleasant note to the soup.

4. Prepare some nice big and chunky croutons from the slice of bread and fry in butter. The later these are cooked the better and they are more delicious hot. At Chez Bruce we cook them to order and serve them straight from the pan. Don't underestimate the quality of a freshly cooked crouton!

5. When the potatoes are thoroughly cooked, season the soup, add a

good glug of double cream – about a coffee cup – and draw off the heat.

6. Make sure the haddock is free of skin and bones and slip gently into the soup. It will not take long to cook.

7. Poach the eggs and add the chives to the soup when the haddock is cooked (after about 5 minutes). The seasoning of this soup is crucial, so check again before serving.

8. Divide the haddock between 4 heated soup plates and pour the soup over. Top with a poached egg and the croutons.

BRUCE POOLE

SLOW ROAST SHOULDER OF LAMB WITH SPICED RICE PILAF, HUMMUS AND YOGHURT

SERVES 4–5 (WITH PLENTY OF RICE LEFT OVER FOR SERVING THE FOLLOWING DAY)

1 shoulder of lamb on the bone
olive oil
2 cloves garlic, cut into slivers
anchovies (optional)

FOR THE PILAF:
2 big onions, peeled
2 cloves garlic, minced
1 heaped tsp each of ground cumin and allspice
a big pinch of saffron
a pinch of sugar
½ level tsp of harissa or considerably less of ground cayenne pepper
a handful of sultanas
2 or 3 dried apricots, chopped
salt
500g basmati rice
1 lemon
a handful of toasted flaked almonds
1 big bunch of fresh coriander and 1 of mint, chopped

TO SERVE:
1 tub of hummus (supermarket stuff is fine, or make your own by blending drained tinned chickpeas with garlic, harissa, lemon juice, olive oil and salt)
1 tub of best Greek yoghurt

METHOD

1. Bring the lamb to room temperature and rub it with olive oil. Stud generously with slivers of garlic (and anchovies if you like them), season well and put into a hot oven (240°C/Gas mark 9) for 20 minutes.

2. Turn the oven down to 140–150°C/Gas mark 2 and roast for a further 3 hours. Baste occasionally with the copious fat which will render from the shoulder. If the meat is getting a bit dark, cover loosely with foil.

3. Turn the oven off and leave the lamb to rest in the oven for about an hour with the door ajar (the meat should be starting to fall away appetisingly from the bone). Alternatively, if time is pressing, roast the shoulder as you would normally, but it will still require good resting.

4. For the pilaf, it is important to select a deep, heavy pan with a tight fitting lid. I use a battered old Le Creuset.

5. Slice thinly or chop the onions and sweat gently in a good slug of olive oil until softened and sweet – about 20 minutes.

6. Now turn up the flame, add a little more oil and begin to fry the onions. Add the garlic, cumin, allspice, saffron, the sugar and the cayenne. It is important to fry these spices well and scrape the bottom of the pan as you go to prevent them catching. Do this for about 5 minutes.

7. Add the dried fruit and plenty of salt, remembering that the pilaf will need lots of seasoning. Add the rice and mix well. Add 600ml of water and as soon as the pilaf comes back to the boil turn right down to the gentlest simmer and cover.

8. After 12 minutes turn off the heat. Do not be tempted to lift off the lid! Leave for at least half an hour to cook through in its own steam. Believe me, it will retain its residual heat.

BRUCE POOLE

179

9. Carve or pull the meat from the shoulder bone. It is impossible to do this elegantly so don't worry unduly. Remove the lid from the pilaf (enjoying the aromas as you do so) and stir the rice well to separate the grains. The rice should be completely dry but cooked — check it for seasoning. Add a generous squeeze of lemon juice, probably half a lemon's worth, the almonds and the chopped coriander and mint.

10. Serve the lamb with the pilaf, hummus and yoghurt, which eats well with the lamb fat. Some roast tomatoes and grilled aubergines would also be good with this.

VANILLA CUSTARD WITH RASPBERRIES

SERVES 4

1 punnet raspberries
600ml double cream
1 vanilla pod
6 egg yolks
50g caster sugar

Make at least 2–3 hours before serving.

METHOD

1. Divide the raspberries between 4 ramekins.

2. Bring the cream to the boil, together with the sliced vanilla pod and all its scraped out seeds. (The dimensions of the pan are quite important here. You need a pan big enough to hold all the ingredients whilst whisking, but not so big that the cream is lost at the bottom. Ideally the cream should be no less than 10cm deep in the pan.)

3. Whisk the egg yolks with the sugar, then pour the boiling cream and vanilla mixture onto the yolks. Return the whole lot back to the pan and put back on to the (lowered) flame.

4. Now here you have to pay attention. Cook the custard, whisking gently in a circular fashion all the while, and watch it very carefully. As it cooks, the speed at which the custard moves around the pan will slow as it thickens slightly but perceptibly. When plenty of steam is given off and the custard revolves less than once around the pan when whisked, (my method of checking for doneness – a thermometer should read 84°C, but I never use one), move quickly and pass the whole lot through a sieve into a big jug or some such container. If you see biggish air bubbles on top that is fine, but if there is a fine eggy scum on top then you have not cooked it enough and it will not set.

BRUCE POOLE

5. Pour the custard over the raspberries, just enough to cover them. You will have some custard left over. No matter as it is delicious on its own and it is difficult to make less than a pint.

6. Refrigerate the custard for a couple of hours or overnight. Serve with whatever biscuit takes your fancy. Shortbread is good.

Joël Robuchon

Chicker Liver Terrine with
  Juniper
Fillet of Beef in Brioche
Soufflé Chartreuse

CHICKEN LIVER TERRINE WITH JUNIPER

SERVES 4

750g chicken livers
450g pork neck (boneless)
100g trompettes de mort mushrooms (optional)
12g fine salt
10g caster sugar
1g pepper
2g ground coriander
2g finely chopped juniper berries
2 sprigs of fresh thyme
pork caul

METHOD

1. Soak the pork caul in cold water for about an hour.

2. Quickly wash the mushrooms under running water. Chop them finely and sauté them for a couple of minutes over high heat until they have given up their juices.

3. Mince the chicken livers and the pork.

4. Mix together all the ingredients, including a few thyme leaves, apart from the caul.

5. Lay the caul along the bottom of a terrine and pile the chicken liver stuffing on top of it. Place the sprigs of thyme on top and then close up the caul.

6. Preheat the oven to 200°C/Gas mark 6.

7. Put a little water into an oven tray, place a cloth on top and then lay the terrine dish on top of that. Bring the water to the boil on the stove then put the whole tray into the oven. Let it cook for 1 hour 30 minutes.

8. Take the terrine out of the oven and let it cool. Refrigerate for 2/3 days before serving.

FILLET OF BEEF IN BRIOCHE

SERVES 6–8

1kg beef fillet
peanut oil
70g butter
2 shallots, diced
1 clove of garlic, crushed
300g diced mushrooms
10g crustless bread, crumbed
30g single cream
a soupspoonful of chopped flat-leaf parsley
500g brioche dough
4 crêpes
1 egg, beaten
1 lump of sugar
I glass of port
200ml cold veal stock
salt and freshly ground black pepper

METHOD

1. Place a small amount of the peanut oil and 20g butter into a pan big enough to hold the fillet and heat until hot. Place the fillet in the pan and brown swiftly on all sides. Place on a rack and leave to rest.

2. In a high-sided frying pan place 30g of cold butter, the diced shallots and the garlic along with a little salt and sweat for about 2–3 minutes without allowing the shallot or garlic to colour.

3. Add the mushrooms and some salt and pepper and cook for about 3 minutes.

4. Add the breadcrumbs and the cream and check the seasoning. Add a soupspoonful of the chopped parsley. Put to one side.

5. Spread out two of the crêpes allowing them to overlap a little and then coat them with some of the mushroom duxelles. Lay the beef on the duxelles, season the fillet and then coat with the remaining mushrooms. Cover with the two remaining crêpes and fold over the edges ensuring the beef is completely enclosed. Place in the fridge.

6. Roll out the brioche pastry to form a large rectangle. Preheat the oven to 220°C/Gas mark 7.

7. Lay the beef on the rolled out pastry and gently enclose it taking care to ensure the dough is pressed together on all sides.

8. Place the fillet on an oven tray and glaze with the beaten egg across the entire surface.

9. Put it into the oven and let it cook for 30 minutes — longer if you like it well-done.

10. To make the port sauce, put the sugar into a heavy bottom casserole dish until it begins to caramelise, then stir. Add the port and let it reduce until just two soupspoonfuls remain. Add the veal stock and bring to the boil and then gently incorporate the rest of the well-chilled butter, cut into small pieces. Season to taste.

11. Take the beef out of the oven when it is golden and allow it to rest for an hour in a warm room. Just before serving put it back into a hot oven for 5 minutes.

12. Carve with an electric knife — it just makes it easier — then add the port sauce. Bon appétit!

SOUFFLÉ CHARTREUSE

SERVES 2

3 eggs, separated
75g caster sugar
25g ricotta
40g 0% fat fromage frais
1 soupspoon of Chartreuse
10g butter, softened
pistachio ice cream, to serve

METHOD

1. Put the egg yolks and 25g of sugar in a bowl and whisk until pale.

2. Incorporate the ricotta and the fromage blanc and place this mixture in the fridge for 2 hours.

3. Heat the oven to 220°C/Gas mark 7.

4. Place the egg whites with the remaining sugar in another bowl and whisk until soft peaks form.

5. Fold together the yolk and cheese mixture and the meringue mixture. Add the Chartreuse.

6. Coat the insides of two ramekins with the butter and spoon in the soufflé mixture evenly.

7. Place the ramekins in the oven and bake for about 8–10 minutes.

8. Take them out of the oven, gently open the top of the soufflés with a spoon and add a scoop of pistachio ice cream.

Michael Romano

Risotto with Eggplant,
  Anchovy and Mint
Halibut Confit
Strawberry Rhubarb
  Pandowdy

RISOTTO WITH AUBERGINE, ANCHOVY AND MINT

Here's a risotto variation whose bold flavours remind us of the food of Rome's Jewish ghetto. Anchovies, Pecorino and mint wake up the subtle, nutty eggplant, which almost melts right into the creamy rice. As a starter this risotto would be a natural before lamb or chicken, or enjoy it as a main course accompanied by a simple salad of bitter greens, like rocket, dandelion or radicchio.

WINE SUGGESTION:

To soften the bitterness of eggplant choose a red wine with ample tannins and fruit. Try a Montepulciano d'Abruzzo or Sardinian canonau from Italy, or from France, a syrah or grenache-based wine from Provence or the Rhône Valley.

SERVES 4

Kosher salt or coarse sea salt
1–2 medium aubergines, unpeeled, cut into
1.5cm dice
5 tbsp plus 2 tbsp extra-virgin olive oil
1.5 litres chicken stock
2 tbsp minced shallots
1 tsp minced garlic
5 anchovy fillets, minced
350g Arborio rice
225ml white wine
3 tbsp chopped fresh mint
3 tbsp butter
50g grated Pecorino Romano
⅛ tsp freshly ground pepper

METHOD

1. Combine 1 quart of cold water and 2 tablespoons salt in a large bowl. Add the diced aubergine and let soak for 30 minutes. Drain well in a colander.

2. In a large sauté pan heat 5tbsp olive oil over medium-high heat until very hot and add the drained aubergine. If your sauté pan is not large enough to hold all the aubergine in a single layer do this step in several batches. Cook the aubergine until well browned and tender — 8 to 10 minutes. Stir often during the last half of cooking and reduce the heat as needed to keep the eggplant from burning. Transfer to a dish and set aside.

3. In a small saucepan bring the chicken stock to a simmer.

4. Combine 2 tablespoons olive oil, the shallots, garlic and anchovy in a 3 litre capacity heavy bottomed saucepan or skillet. Place over medium heat and stir to cook without colouring — about 2 minutes. Add the rice and 1 teaspoon salt, and stir with a wooden spoon until the rice is coated with the oil. Add the wine and bring to a boil over medium-high heat, stirring constantly until the rice absorbs the wine.

5. Ladle 100ml or so of the simmering broth into the saucepan and stir until it is absorbed. Continue with the rest of the broth, adding a ladleful at a time and letting each addition be absorbed completely into the rice before adding more liquid. The constant stirring allows the rice to release its starch into the cooking liquid, resulting in the characteristic risotto creaminess. Count on approximately 20 to 25 minutes for the rice to be cooked al dente.

6. Fold in the aubergine and cook until heated through — about 30 seconds. Add the mint, swirl in the butter and half the cheese and season with ½ teaspoon salt and the pepper. Spoon the risotto onto a warm platter, or individual bowls, sprinkle with the remaining Pecorino and serve immediately.

MICHAEL ROMANO

HALIBUT CONFIT

Poaching halibut in a deep bath of olive oil imbues a rich
Mediterranean flavour to the firm-fleshed white fish that is perfectly
complemented by a quick sauce made from ripe, peak-of-the-season
tomatoes. You'll have a lot of olive oil left over after you "confit" the
halibut. To use it again, either for this recipe or for deep-frying
calamari or other fish, allow the oil to cool, strain and refrigerate in
a tightly covered bottle for up to 2 weeks. As you cook the halibut
keep in mind that you are poaching, not deep-frying, and that the fish
should be very gently simmering in the olive oil. Serve with sautéed
zucchini or green beans.

WINE SUGGESTION:

These flavours suggest a Provençal style wine, like Bandol rosé, St.
Joseph blanc or Condrieu. From California, go with a well made rosé,
sauvignon blanc or marsanne.

SERVES 4

4 tbsp olive oil
6 thinly sliced spring onions (white bulbs and green tops)
or 2 shallots
2 garlic cloves, minced
1kg ripe, fresh tomatoes, peeled, seeded and chopped
2 tsp coarse sea salt
¼ tsp freshly ground black pepper
1½ tsp red wine vinegar
a handful fresh basil leaves, sliced
1 litre extra-virgin olive oil
4 skinless halibut fillets, about 175g each
Kosher salt or coarse sea salt
freshly ground black pepper

METHOD

1. Heat the 4 tbsp oil over a medium flame in a 3 litre capacity, non-reactive saucepan. Add the spring onions and cook, stirring occasionally, until softened but not browned — about 2 minutes. Add the garlic and continue cooking for an additional 2 minutes. Add the tomato and cook, stirring occasionally until juicy — 2 to 3 minutes. Stir in the salt, pepper, vinegar and basil. Simmer for 30 seconds, remove from the heat and set aside.

2. Pour the litre of olive oil into a pot large enough to hold the halibut fillets in 1 layer and deep enough so that the oil comes to no more than one third the way up its sides. Set the pot on the stove, turned to its very lowest heat setting, and heat the oil to 82°–88°C on a deep-fat thermometer.

3. Season the halibut with salt to taste on both sides and sprinkle with pepper on just the underside. Using a spatula carefully slide the fish into the oil and poach until the halibut is just cooked through — 8 to 9 minutes. Remove from the oil with the spatula and drain on paper towels.

4. Return the tomato sauce to a simmer. Divide the sauce among 4 deep plates or large bowls. Set the halibut fillets on top of the sauce and serve hot.

STRAWBERRY RHUBARB PANDOWDY

Beyond being a fabulous word that conjures up the best in classic American desserts, pandowdies are darned good — and easy to make. Actually, a pandowdy is pretty similar to a cobbler, with one small but important distinction: in the middle of baking the crust is cut into pieces and then smooshed down into the fruit filling. While this pandowdy uses the tried and tested coupling of strawberries and rhubarb, you can certainly make it with other fruits when they're in season. Plums, peaches, apricots, apples and pears work particularly well. Serve it piping hot, accompanied by a dollop of country cream, Chantilly cream or a scoop of vanilla ice cream.

SERVES 10–12

FOR THE PIE CRUST:
110g plain flour
110g superfine flour
1 tbsp sugar
¼ tsp salt
110g cold butter, cut into 1.5cm cubes
2 tbs Crisco or other vegetable shortening, cut into 1.5cm cubes and frozen
120ml iced water, plus more if needed

FOR THE FRUIT FILLING:
500g trimmed, rinsed rhubarb, cut into 4cm lengths
350g rinsed and stemmed strawberries
120ml maple syrup
3 tbsp butter, in small pieces
2 tbsp milk
2 tbsp sugar

METHOD

1. To make the dough, place the flours, sugar, salt and chilled butter in the bowl of an electric mixer fitted with the paddle attachment. Mix on the lowest speed, for 30 seconds to a minute, until most of the butter is blended with the flours, but with a few larger lumps of butter still visible. Add the frozen pieces of shortening and mix slowly for another 30 seconds to a minute, until the dough is crumbly with some small lumps of butter and shortening remaining.

2. Still mixing on low speed, pour in the iced water and blend for a few seconds, until the dough just comes together. Scoop the dough onto a sheet of clingfilmand press into a smooth disk; wrap tightly and refrigerate for at least an hour, or up to 2 days.

3. Preheat the oven to 220°C/Gas mark 7.

4. In a mixing bowl gently toss the rhubarb pieces and strawberries with the maple syrup. Then spread an even layer of the fruit into a 25cm by 33cm Pyrex baking dish or cake pan. Dot the top with the bits of butter.

5. On a floured work surface roll the chilled dough into an even rectangle, about 3mm thick, until it is the same size as the pan. To transfer the dough, roll it up on a dough pin and then unroll it over the fruit. Trim any excess dough, brush the crust with the milk and sprinkle evenly with the sugar. Pierce a dozen small steam vents in the dough with the tip of a paring knife.

6. Bake for 40 minutes or until the crust has started to turn golden brown. Remove the pan from the oven and slice the crust lengthways into 4 even strips, then slice crosswise to divide the crust into 16 small rectangles. With an offset spatula (such as a pancake turner) push the pieces of crust down into the bubbling fruit juices. Bake for another 30 minutes or so until the crust becomes a deep golden brown and the fruit has thickened.

7. Serve the pandowdy warm, spooned into dessert dishes, with the browned crust showing.

MICHAEL ROMANO

Rick Stein

Duck Liver Parfait...
Salmon en Croute...
Steamed Treacle Sponge...

DUCK LIVER PARFAIT WITH ONION CONFIT AND WALNUT BREAD TOAST

SERVES 10–12

450g duck livers, trimmed of any white sinews
1 garlic clove, crushed
2 tbsp port
1 tbsp brandy
225g unsalted butter, melted and cooled slightly
salt and freshly ground white pepper

FOR THE ONION CONFIT:
100g butter
700g onions, peeled and thinly sliced
75g granulated sugar
7 tbsp sherry vinegar
225ml red wine
Salt and freshly ground black pepper

thin slices of lightly toasted walnut bread to serve

METHOD

1. Preheat the oven to 110°C/Gas mark ½. Put the duck livers, 1 tsp of salt, 20 turns of white pepper, garlic, port and brandy into a food processor and blend for 1 minute until smooth. Add the cooled melted butter and then press the mixture through a fine sieve into a bowl.

2. Pour the mixture into a 450g loaf tin lined with cooking grade cling film, cover with a sheet of lightly buttered foil and put it into a roasting tin half-filled with hot water. Transfer to the oven and cook for 1¼ hours. Remove from the roasting tin, leave to cool, then remove the foil, re-cover with cling film and leave to chill overnight.

3. For the onion confit, heat the butter in a large pan until a light nut brown. Add the onions and sugar and cook slowly for about 45 minutes, stirring now and then, until the onions are very soft and richly caramelised. Add the sherry vinegar and red wine and cook for a further 10 minutes, stirring now and then, until the mixture has reduced and thickened and turned a dark mahogany colour. Stir in 1 teaspoon of salt and 1 teaspoon of black pepper and leave to cool, but don't chill.

4. To serve, uncover the parfait and invert it onto a board. Peel off the cling film and cut the parfait across into approximately 5mm thick slices. You don't want them to be too thick as it's very rich. Put a slice of the parfait slightly to one side of each plate and spoon a heaped tablespoon of the onion confit alongside. Serve with the walnut bread toast.

SALMON EN CROUTE WITH TARRAGON BUTTER AND WILTED SPINACH

SERVES 8

**2 x 550g pieces of thick salmon fillet, skinned, cut from
behind the gut cavity of a 3–4kg fish. Each should measure
about 20 cm long
500g spinach, large stalks removed, washed and dried well
2 x 500g packets fresh puff pastry
1 egg, beaten
2 tablespoons vegetable oil to grease baking sheets
salt and freshly ground black pepper.**

**FOR THE TARRAGON BUTTER:
100g unsalted butter, softened
1 tablespoon chopped tarragon
½ teaspoon salt
1 tablespoon lemon juice**

METHOD

1. Trim the salmon fillets if necessary so that they are the same size.

Season each piece with ¼ teaspoon of salt and some black pepper.
Beat the ingredients for the tarragon butter together in a bowl.

2. Heat 1 tablespoon of the tarragon butter in a large pan. Add a
large handful of the spinach and as soon as it starts to wilt down
into the bottom of the pan, add more spinach until it is all in the
pan. Cook for 1 minute over a high heat, then tip into a colander and
press out as much of the excess liquid as you can. Transfer to a
board and coarsely chop. Season to taste with salt and pepper and
leave to cool.

3. Cut a 350g piece from one block of pastry (saving the rest for
another dish) and roll out on a lightly floured surface into a

rectangle 4cm bigger than the salmon fillets, about 20x30cm.

Roll out the second piece of pastry into a rectangle 5cm larger than the first one, approximately 25x35cm.

4. Lay the smaller rectangle of pastry on a well-greased baking sheet and spread half of the spinach mixture in the centre to form a rectangle the same size as the salmon. Put one of the salmon fillets on top, skinned-side down, and spread with the rest of the tarragon butter. Cover with the second fillet, skinned-side up this time and cover with the rest of the spinach, trying to make sure that the spinach covers the salmon in an even layer.

5. Brush a wide band of beaten egg around the salmon, and lay the second piece of pastry on top, taking care not to stretch it, and trying to ensure that you have not trapped in too much air. Tuck the pastry in well around the salmon and press the edges together to seal, then trim away the excess pastry to leave a 2.5cm band all the way around. Mark the edge with a fork and then chill in the fridge for 1 hour.

6. Preheat the oven to 200°C/Gas mark 6. Brush the salmon parcel with beaten egg and chill for another 5 minutes, then remove and brush once more with egg – this will give it a nice, deeply golden glaze. Then score the surface of the pastry into a tight diamond pattern with the tip of a small, sharp knife. Bake for 35–40 minutes.

7. Remove the salmon parcel from the oven and leave it to rest for 5 minutes. Then cut it across into 2.5cm slices to serve.

STEAMED TREACLE SPONGE WITH BUTTERSCOTCH SAUCE AND CUSTARD

SERVES 8

175g softened butter, plus a little extra for greasing
175g light muscovado sugar
1 tbsp black treacle
3 large eggs
175g self-raising flour

FOR THE BUTTERSCOTCH SAUCE:
50g butter
75g light muscovado sugar
25g Demerara sugar
150g golden syrup
150ml double cream

FOR THE CUSTARD:
1 vanilla pod
600ml full cream milk
4 egg yolks
3 tbsp caster sugar
4 tsp cornflour

METHOD

1. Generously grease a 1.2 litre pudding basin with some butter. Cream the butter in a bowl until light and creamy. Add the muscovado sugar and beat vigorously until the mixture is pale and fluffy, then beat in the black treacle. Beat in the eggs, one at a time, adding a large spoonful of the flour with the last egg, and then gently fold in the rest of the flour.

2. Spoon the mixture into the pudding basin and lightly level the top of the mixture. Cover the bowl with a pleated sheet of buttered foil and tie in place with string.

3. Bring a 5cm depth of water to the boil in a large pan containing some sort of shallow trivet in the base. Add the pudding, cover and steam for 2 hours.

4. Meanwhile, make the butterscotch sauce. Put the butter, muscovado and Demerara sugars and golden syrup into a pan and leave over a low heat, stirring now and then, until the sugars have dissolved. Stir in the double cream and keep warm.

5. For the custard, slit open the vanilla pod and scrape out the seeds with the tip of a sharp knife. Put the milk, vanilla pod and seeds into a non-stick pan and bring to the boil. Remove the pan from the heat and set aside for 20 minutes or so to allow the flavour of vanilla to infuse the milk. Cream the egg yolks, sugar and cornflour together in a bowl until smooth. Bring the milk back to the boil, remove the vanilla pod and gradually beat the milk into the egg yolk mixture. Return to the pan and cook over a medium heat, stirring constantly until the custard thickens, but don't let the mixture boil.

6. To serve, uncover the pudding and carefully run a knife around the edge of the basin. Cover with an inverted plate and turn it out. Pour over some of the hot butterscotch sauce and serve cut into wedges with the custard and the rest of the sauce.

From Rick Stein's Food Heroes, published by BBC Books. Used by permission of The Random House Group Ltd.

Alice Waters

Persimmon and Pomegranate
 Salad
Braised Short Ribs
Potato Parsnip Purée
Cranberry Upside-Down Cake

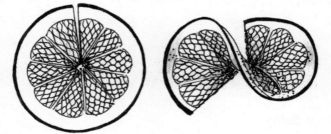

PERSIMMON AND POMEGRANATE SALAD

There are 2 varieties of persimmon available on the market, fuyu and hachiya. Fuyu are round and flat and are eaten while still crisp; they make colourful and tasty salads. Hachiya are elongated with a pointy tip and are quite tannic until ripe and very, very soft.

SERVES 4

3 ripe medium fuyu persimmons
½ pomegranate
1 tbsp sherry or red wine vinegar
salt and freshly-ground black pepper
3 tbsp extra-virgin olive oil

METHOD

1. Cut the tops from and peel the persimmons.

2. Slice them thinly or cut into small wedges, removing any seeds you find. Arrange the wedges on a plate.

3. Hold the pomegranate cut-side down, over a bowl: Pound on the back of the fruit with a large spoon to dislodge the seeds. Pick out and discard any white pith that may have fallen out with the seeds. Sprinkle the seeds over the persimmon wedges.

4. Mix together the vinegar, salt and pepper. Stir to dissolve the salt and then whisk in the olive oil. Taste and correct the salt and acid as needed. Spoon the vinaigrette over the fruit and serve.

VARIATIONS:

1. Toast 3 tablespoons of walnuts in a preheated 190°C/Gas mark 5 oven for 8 minutes. While they are still warm rub the walnuts in a clean tea towel to remove some of the skins. Crumble the toasted walnuts over the fruit before dressing the salad.

2. Toss 4 small handfuls of lettuce with half the vinaigrette. (I prefer lettuces such as rocket, frisée, escarole, radicchio or chicory.) Arrange the lettuce on the plate and then arrange the fruit and nuts, if using, over the lettuce. Pour the rest of the vinaigrette over.

BRAISED SHORT RIBS WITH POTATO PARSNIP PURÉE

Braising short ribs on the bone makes one of the most succulent meat dishes there is. (In the UK 'short ribs' are usually sold as a rolled rib joint. Ask your butcher for beef ribs cut from either the rib or shoulder end, and left on the bone.)

SERVES 4

1.5kg beef ribs, cut into 5cm pieces
salt and freshly-ground black pepper
1 tbsp olive oil
2 small onions, peeled and quartered
2 carrots, peeled and cut in large pieces
1 celery stalk, peeled and quartered
6 garlic cloves, peeled and coarsely chopped
6 thyme sprigs
4 parsley sprigs
1 bay leaf
3 tomatoes, cored and quartered
170ml red wine
500ml chicken or beef stock

METHOD

1. Season the ribs a day in advance if possible. Cover and refrigerate until an hour before cooking.

2. Preheat the oven to 230°C/Gas mark 8.

3. Place the ribs in a roasting pan in a single layer, bone-side down. Roast for about 25 to 30 minutes to brown the meat and render some of the fat. Remove from the oven, pour off the fat, and set the pan of ribs aside.

4. While the short ribs are roasting, cook the vegetables.

5. Heat the olive oil in a large heavy based frying pan and add all the vegetables and aromatics.

6. Cook over medium heat, stirring occasionally, for 10 minutes.

7. Add the tomatoes and cook for 5 minutes longer. Pour in the wine and the stock and bring to a simmer.

8. Remove the ribs from the roasting pan and pour the contents of the frying pan into the pan.

9. Place the ribs on top of the vegetables, bone-side up. Cover tightly with a lid or foil.

10. Put the pan back in the hot oven. After about 20 minutes, when the liquid just begins to bubble, lower the heat to 160°C/Gas mark 3, and loosen the lid or foil to release some of the heat so the liquid doesn't boil.

11. Continue braising the ribs until the meat is very tender and begins to fall off the bones, about another 1 to 1½ hours. Lift the ribs out of the braising liquid and set aside.

12. Strain the liquid, pressing down with the back of a spoon on the aromatic vegetables to extract all the juices. Discard the vegetables.

13. Allow the braising liquid to settle and skim off the fat. Taste the liquid; if it has reduced too much or is a little salty you may need to add a splash of water. Reheat the ribs in the braising liquid just before serving.

POTATO PARSNIP PURÉE

SERVES 4

500g Desirée potatoes, peeled and cut into medium-size pieces.
250g parsnips, peeled and cut into chunks
120ml whole milk (or potato cooking water, see below)
4 tbsp butter, cut into pieces
salt

METHOD

1. Boil the potatoes in well salted water, for 15–20 minutes, until fully cooked through.

2. In a separate pot, boil the parsnips.

3. Test the potatoes by cutting a piece in half and checking the centre. It should be tender, flaky and dry. Drain the potatoes well, retaining the cooking water, and leave them in the colander to steam for a few minutes.

4. Repeat for the parsnips.

5. Meanwhile, in the now empty pot, heat the milk or water from cooking the potatoes.

6. Return the drained potatoes and parsnips to the pot and add the butter. With a potato masher or a wooden spoon, mash the potatoes and parsnips over low heat, to keep them hot. Season with: salt to taste.

7. Add more milk or potato water if the purée is too stiff.

CRANBERRY UPSIDE-DOWN CAKE

This cake is very versatile and can be made with apples, pears, peaches, plums or any full-flavoured, slightly acidic fruit.

MAKES ONE 20CM ROUND CAKE OR ONE 20CM SQUARE CAKE

55g unsalted butter
150g brown sugar
250g fresh cranberries
60ml orange juice
2 eggs, separated, at room temperature
120ml whole milk, at room temperature
175g unbleached all-purpose flour
2 tsp baking powder
¼ tsp of salt
110g unsalted butter, softened
200g sugar
1 tsp vanilla extract

METHOD

1. Preheat the oven to 180°C/Gas mark 4.

2. Put the butter and sugar into a heavy based pan or heavy-duty cake pan and cook over medium heat, stirring constantly, until the butter melts and starts to bubble. Remove from the heat and allow to cool.

3. Heat the cranberries and orange juice in a small saucepan and cook until the cranberries just start to pop. Remove from the heat and pour evenly over the cooled caramel.

4. Beat the butter and sugar until light and fluffy. Beat in the egg yolks one at a time and stir in the vanilla.

5. Sift together the flour, baking powder and salt, and add to the egg

mixture alternately with the milk, starting and ending with one-third of the flour. Stir just until the flour is incorporated.

6. Whisk the egg whites until they hold soft peaks.

7. Fold one-third of the egg whites into the batter and then gently fold in the rest. Pour the batter over the cranberries in the pan and smooth the top with a spatula.

8. Bake for 30–35 minutes or until the top is golden brown and the cake pulls away from the sides of the pan.

Remove from the oven and allow the cake to cool for 15 minutes. Run a knife around the edge of the pan and invert the cake onto a serving plate.

Jancis Robinson

Entertaining with Wine

WHAT IS WINE?

Wine is quite simply the most delicious, most varied and most complex drink on the planet. *I* think.

To me it is almost incredible that the fermented juice of a single fruit, the grape, can offer us so many different styles of liquid. From the tingly, zesty, water-white, light and lively to the rich, purple-black, mellow and full-bodied. It comes both still and fizzy and at all points in between. It can be bone dry or tooth-rottingly sweet.

The job of the wine producer is to ripen healthy grapes in the vineyard, full of grape sugar that can, by the action of yeast in the atmosphere, be fermented into alcohol. If all the grape sugar is fermented, the wine will be dry, and enlivened by the acidity that is naturally present in grapes. The more grape sugar fermented into alcohol, the more potent the wine will be. Wine can vary from less than 8 to more than 15 percent alcohol, with 13.5 being about average.

Perhaps wine's real distinguishing mark, the thing that sets it apart from other drinks, is the ability of the best wines to last for decades and sometimes centuries – not just lasting but improving. I have been lucky enough to taste wines up to 200 years old that were still totally thrilling and alive. Nothing else that we consume is capable of remaining healthy and evolving over such a long period.

But it's not just history that is important to wine. Geography is absolutely crucial. Wine is one of the very, very few things we can pluck off a shelf and know precisely which spot on the globe was responsible for it. Sometimes the label will carry the name of a fairly big region such as South Eastern Australia, or Bordeaux. But generally the smaller the area nominated, Barossa Valley, say, or Pauillac, the less likely the wine will be blended from lots of different vineyards and may well be the produce of a single vineyard.

More than that, it may well be the produce of a single person, whose name is also often on the label. So for the more artisanal lines produced today, there are strong parallels between books and wine – these are personally authored products.

I see many similarities between specialist bookshops and specialist wine stores too. They tend to be run by real enthusiasts who like nothing better than giving advice. If you want to learn more about wine, find a local retailer and tell them what sort of wine you think you like. It is in their interests to help you find more examples, perhaps suggesting something that is a little bit more exciting than what you are used to.

The articles which will follow provide a comprehensive guide to tasting, choosing, serving, storing and describing wine, getting the most from each bottle. I hope very much they will help you to enjoy wine even more – perhaps even as much as I do.

HOW TO BECOME A WINE TASTER

All you need to be a wine taster is a glass and a moment's attention. A lot of unnecessary fuss is made about extraneous smells (taking that argument to its logical conclusion we'd never serve food with wine) and about the condition of the palate. Some foods seriously distract from the taste of wine, but a mouthful of water or neutral food such as bread is enough to neutralise the palate after all but the fiercest chilli. A more serious enemy to wine is toothpaste; many's the glass of champagne that has been wasted because of tooth brushing immediately before drinking it. Non-minty mouthwashes can freshen the palate without immobilising it.

STEP 1

Looking at wine is the least important (and least pleasurable) part of wine tasting — although it can be immensely useful to someone trying to guess the identity of a mystery wine, so-called 'blind tasting'. Tilting the glass away from you, preferably against a white background, exposes the different shades of colour (the more the better), especially at the rim where the age of a wine tends to show. The browner a wine the older it usually is. Red wines tend to go from deep purple to pale tawny, while whites go from pale greenish yellow to deep gold. In very general terms, the best wines actually have a luscious sheen to them, while commercial, heavily treated ones can look dull and monotone. Note: some wine professionals hold wine glasses by the base, but holding them by the stem is much easier and keeps the wine equally unaffected by your body heat.

STEP 2

The importance of smelling the wine is outlined in Our Sense of Taste. Since a wine's flavour molecules are given off only on the liquid's surface, they can be seriously encouraged by maximising the wine's surface area. This is done by swirling the wine round in a glass, ideally with a stem so that a graceful movement, which has no effect on the wine's temperature, can be achieved, preferably no more than half-full so that no wine is spilt. The ideal wine glass goes in towards the rim so that swirled wine tends to stay in the glass and so does the heady vapour above it. Just one short sniff while you concentrate is enough. Notice whether the smell is clean and attractive (if not, either reject the wine as faulty or deliberately avoid smelling it as you drink!); how intense the smell is; and what the smell reminds you of. Grapes contain thousands of compounds, many of which are also found in other familiar substances. Furthermore, the processes of fermentation and maturation can add their own layers of flavour as different compounds interact. The aroma from the grape is known as a primary aroma, that from the winemaking secondary and those aromas associated with the ageing process are called tertiary.

It is not surprising, in the light of all the influences on the aroma of a wine, that words are poor descriptors of something as subtle, subjective and private as smell perceptions. The best we can do to describe the smell, or flavour, of a wine is list those things of which it reminds us. There may be many thousands of other substances in wine which have no direct counterpart elsewhere, or which are too obscure to have their own name. Flavour compounds – the monoterpenes found in florally aromatic grapes and the green pepper – like methoxypyrazine found in Sauvignon Blanc and Cabernet Sauvignon, for example – have been energetically researched by the wine industry. See tasting terms for some more guidance on how to apply words to the very varied smells of different wines.

STEP 3

Take a mouthful of wine and try to ensure that all of the palate, or at least all of the tongue, is exposed to the liquid, the better to gauge the dimensions that can be sensed in the mouth. Notice how sweet, sour/acid, bitter, tannic/astringent, alcoholic and gassy the wine is, as explained in The Sense of Taste. Try to gauge the wine's body, i.e. how unlike water it is. It also helps draw vapour up the retro-nasal passage that links the back of the mouth with the nose if a little air is taken in to the mouth at the same time (which is why professional wine tasters can look and sound so disgusting). Then comes the great divide between tasting for work or play: workers (who may have to taste 100 wines a day) spit while players, thank goodness, swallow.

STEP 4

Now is the moment to try to assess the wine as a whole. Were the dimensions of sweetness, acidity, alcohol and the possible elements of bitterness, tannin and gassiness in balance, or did one of them obtrude? In young red wines, for example, tannin often dominates, while young whites are often very acid. This lack of balance would be a fault in an older wine. Was the sweetness counterbalanced by acidity or did it taste sickly?

The other great indicator of quality is length – how long did the impact of the wine last after you swallowed it? Many a mediocre wine leaves no trace either on the palate or in the olfactory area, whereas a mouthful of really fine wine can continue to reverberate for 30 seconds or more after it disappeared down the throat.

SOME TASTING EXERCISES

Put a clothes peg or diving clip on your nose, and see whether you can tell black coffee from black tea. Blindfold, you probably couldn't tell milk chocolate from cheddar cheese. All of this demonstrates just how important the nose is in identifying flavour.

To work out how your palate reacts to acidity, smell and then taste lemon juice or vinegar. It takes only a smell to make the sides of my tongue start to crinkle up, but different tasters react differently. Acid also tends to make the mouth water.

To identify tannin in wine, rinse a mouthful of cold black tea round your palate and notice which parts of your mouth react most dramatically. The insides of my cheeks pucker up. (Notice how you can't smell tannin, or sugar, however.)

To get some idea of body as it relates to wine, notice the difference in palate impact between a light-bodied Mosel (German wine in a tall green bottle) with an alcohol content of less than 10 percent and a full-bodied Chardonnay or white Rhône wine with an alcoholic content of more than 13.5 percent. Notice in particular how unlike water the latter is, and how it may leave a hot, sweet sensation on the palate (alcohol often tastes sweet).

BECOMING A WINE TASTER

I believe that anyone with a sense of smell and an interest in wine can become a wine taster, and that it takes hardly any time at all. I am bolstered in this belief by memories of the very first professional wine tasting I went to. Hugh Johnson was there, and the editor of Decanter magazine, and, horror of horrors, we all had to sit round a table and opine. I carefully watched what they did (much slurping and spitting) and copied them, while keeping very quiet indeed. But after listening to them all trying to describe the same wines and doing it with completely different and sometimes contradictory words, I realised that applying words to wine is a complete free-for-all.

No one other than you can know exactly how a wine strikes your senses. There are no rights or wrongs in wine appreciation and no absolutes when it comes to tasting terms, so the opinion of the novice is every bit as valuable as that of the expert. The only difference is that the expert has been allowed to gain self-confidence, so we propound our theories rather more loudly than most newcomers.

In fact I often find that novice tasters are much better at coming up with the perfect word to describe a wine flavour than us professionals who used up our tasting vocabulary years ago. (Débutantes can even be better at blind tasting than professionals, partly because they have tasted fewer confusing exceptions to the rule, and also because less is expected of them.) Wine tasting is the definitive subjective sport. Once you have consciously tasted a few wines, you can build on that experience by starting to notice the common characteristics of the wines you like.

Putting that together with the profiles of different grape varieties (in most cases the dominant factor in shaping how a wine tastes) should help you pick out the sort of wines that happen to appeal to your palate.

SCORING WINE

Professional wine judges often give wines points out of 100, 20 or 10 because they are expected to come up with a ranking of how a group of wines showed on a given day. It might amuse you to keep written notes and to append scores to them. For my own interest I try to make a record of a wine's state of maturity, using arrows in different directions – or giving a suggested period during which I think the wine will be at its best ("Drink 2010-18", for instance, is the sort of suggestion I give, with my scores out of 20, with all my thousands of tasting notes).

Many wine critics and wine publications publish wine scores, which can be useful summaries of how the particular bottles tasted showed to that particular taster on the day of the tasting. Wine changes so unpredictably, however (and different casks and even bottles vary), and wine preferences are so subjective, that it is important not to be mesmerised by the apparent precision of these ratings. Find a wine critic whose taste you share and follow his or her recommendations, but not slavishly, please. Always remember that wine critics tend to taste dozens of wine at a time, so the flashy ones get the highest scores. The saddest thing I ever heard was when my most intelligent, wine-loving friend reported, crestfallen, about a wine tasted the previous evening, "I really enjoyed it, but I looked it up in Parker [the powerful American wine critic] and he only gave it an 83." Have confidence in your own judgements. They are the only ones that need matter to you.

HOW TO SERVE WINE

For me, choosing the right wine to serve on a particular occasion is almost as thrilling as the wine itself — perverse at that may seem. It gives me real pleasure to feel that the bottle, or bottles, have been just right for the circumstances, the people, the time and any food that's served at the same time.

It is usually a waste, and entirely inappropriate, for example, to think that the more you spend on wine the more it will please. Typically, the most expensive bottles in a wine shop are tough little babies in terms of their evolution: mute, scrunched-up bundles of ingredients that have many years' bottle maturation before they will begin to prove, in mellow middle age, why they were worth paying through the nose for.

And there is a place and a time for everything — even the fanciest bottle of wine. I shall never forget that the first time I ever tasted the fabulous Château Cheval Blanc 1947 was at an outdoor lunch in a sunny Suffolk garden where the breeze playfully wafted into the hot, blue sky every nuance of its subtle bouquet.

A well-chilled, flavourful dry rosé would probably have been just the thing for this outdoor lunch — and yet it would probably taste extremely dreary at an urban dinner party in midwinter.

Other examples of the right bottles in the wrong place include:

Mosel Riesling with hearty stews

New Zealand Sauvignon served to any but the most cosmopolitan native of Sancerre

Heavy Chardonnay at lunchtime

Tough, tannic young reds served to wine debutantes

Châteauneuf-du-Pape drunk in midsummer in Châteauneuf-du-Pape (or indeed most full-bodied, alcoholic reds in the heat of the summer that is responsible for that alcohol)

HOW TO CHOOSE

It is worth trying to match a wine's:

quality level

style

flavour

geographical origins

to:

people – take account of individuals' likes, dislikes, prejudices and capacities for alcohol

occasion – whether it's the most casual encounter or a formal celebration may influence the most appropriate price level

weather – the ambient temperature and humidity level can have an enormous effect on what sort of wines taste best (see below)

time of day – may be a significant factor as far as alcohol intake is concerned

place – inside or outside? Is more than one wine appropriate, or feasible?

food – see Matching Wine and Food for more on this.

TEMPERATURE – THE CRUCIAL ELEMENT

It is impossible to over-estimate the effect of serving temperatures on how a wine will taste. Serving a wine at the most flattering temperature may seem absurdly high-falutin' and precious as an activity, but it really can transform ink into velvet and, conversely, zest into flab. (Unlike the wine itself, it need not cost anything either . . .)

The principles are delightfully simple:

1. The cooler the wine the less it will smell.

2. The warmer the wine the more smelly it will be.

3. Low temperatures emphasise acidity and tannin.

4. High temperatures minimise them.

The corollary of rule 1 is that if you find yourself with a wine that tastes (i.e. smells) truly horrid, but you have to serve or drink it, then chill it to pieces. (If it's a full-bodied red such as shiraz, zinfandel, cabernet sauvignon, Châteauneuf du Pape, Barolo, it could be difficult to pull this off — you'll just have to boil off the flavour and serve it, with added spice and sugar, as mulled wine.

Rule 1 also means that the more naturally aromatic a wine (Riesling, Sauvignon Blanc, Cabernet Franc, Gamay for example), the cooler you can afford to serve it — a useful observation if you need the refreshment of a cool drink. Sparkling wines also show quite well at low temperatures, which slow the release of carbon dioxide.

Rule 2 means that full-bodied wines, as above, whose natural extract tends to make it difficult for flavour molecules to escape to deliver messages to the olfactory area, can be served much warmer than lighter wines. This applies every bit as much to whites as to reds. The limit to this rule is reached when the serving temperature rises above 20°C and an increasing proportion of compounds are literally boiled off.

Rule 3 means that you can make a flabby wine taste infinitely better by chilling it a little. Thus, all but the most perfectly balanced sweet wine benefit from being chilled, as do many red burgundies, and soft red wines such as Beaujolais, which could do with a bit of artificially encouraged structure.

Rule 4 is particularly useful because it means that young red wines, and also the full-bodied ones listed above, which would seem almost hideously tough when served slightly cool, can be immeasurably improved by serving them on the warm side.

ROUGH GUIDE AS TO SUITABLE SERVING TEMPERATURES:

Wine style	Ideal serving temperature °C/F	Practical advice refrigerator for (hrs):
Light, sweet, whites	5-10/40-50	4+
Sparkling whites	6-10/42-50	4
Light (aromatic) dry whites	8-12/46-54	2
Sparkling reds	10-12/50-54	1.5
Medium bodied, dry whites	10-12/50-54	1.5
Full sweet whites	8-12/46-54	2
Light reds	10-12/50-54	1.5
Full dry whites	12-16/54-60	1
Medium reds	14-17/57-63	-
Full or tannic reds	15-18/59-65	-

NB Throughout, rosés behave as slightly fuller bodied equivalent whites.

WHICH WINES ARE WORTH AGEING

WHETHER TO STORE WINE

Wine, like any fresh food, changes with time. But whereas most consumables deteriorate from the moment we buy them, wine is one of the very few things we buy regularly that has the capacity to change for the better. Perhaps the top 10 percent of all reds and five percent of all whites (and those are generous estimates) will be more pleasurable and more interesting to drink when they are five years old than at one year old.

The top one percent of all wine made has the ability to improve for a decade or two or, in some cases, even more. The great majority of all wine, however, will actually start to lose the fruitiness that gives it youthful appeal within six months of being bottled. But how is the poor old consumer to identify which bottles to store lovingly and which to consume as fast as he or she possibly can?

The supermarkets, to give them credit, have in recent years responded quite well to this problem. Many back labels on their own bottlings give specific advice on when to open them (typically 'within six months to a year of purchase'). But it can be extremely difficult to get reliable advice on when to open finer wines. How many people realise, for example, that the most expensive bottles of red wine in a store are probably those least likely to give pleasure that evening – because they are the ones with a long life expectancy which have been stacked full of mouth-puckering, inky tannin and are generally commercially available only in their youth?

The most obvious candidates for long-term ageing in bottle are reds made from Cabernet Sauvignon, Cabernet Franc, Merlot, Syrah and Nebbiolo, botrytised sweet wines such as top Sauternes, Loire wines made from the Chenin Blanc grape, most wines made from the Riesling grape and expensive white burgundy.

WHAT HAPPENS WHEN WINE AGES?

The more fruit, acid and phenolics that go into a bottle of wine at the beginning, the more complex interactions there can be between all these compounds and the more rewarding it can be to age that bottle. This means that the less water there is in the grape (and therefore the thicker the grape variety's skins, as a result of a drier growing season or less irrigation used), the more likely it is that the resulting wine will repay cellaring. Tannins and colouring matter known as anthocyanins are the most obvious types of phenolics and what preserves red wine as these interactions occur. These and other compounds continue to interact, forming bigger and bigger complex compounds, which after a few years are too big to remain in solution and are precipitated as sediment. So as good quality, concentrated red wine ages it becomes paler and softer to taste, while gaining considerably in the range of flavours it presents (which by now constitute a bouquet rather than simple aromas). Any red wine with visible sediment is likely to have completed quite a bit of its ageing process. Even less is known about how white wine ages, although acidity is thought to be the preservative white counterpart to tannin.

Certainly, the longest-lived white wines are those with good extract but good acidity too. The fact that white wines have far fewer phenolics explains why fewer of them can last as long in bottle (although botrytis, or 'noble rot', can preserve sweet white wines for decades). Very few rosé wines improve with age, presumably because they tend to have less acidity than white wines and far fewer phenolics than reds.

WINES TO DRINK AS YOUNG AS POSSIBLE

It follows from the section above that the great majority of wines, made to be easy to appreciate in youth, are not worth giving 'bottle age', the jargon for what happens when wine is kept for years in sealed bottles. The economics of producing almost any wine selling for less than about £5/$10 a bottle mean that there is unlikely to be a sufficient concentration of ageable ingredients in that bottle. (The only possible exception to this might be an inexpensive non-irrigated red from an under-developed wine region such as some in Greece, Morocco, Argentina or parts of Spain.) All of the following should usually be drunk within a year of bottling, and ideally even sooner when their youthful fruit is at its most obvious:

table wine (Europe)
jug wine (US)
wine in boxes, cans or tetrapaks
less expensive vins de pays
nouveau/primeur/novella wines
branded wines under £5/$10 — indeed most branded wines
Germany's QbA wines
rosé and blush wines
inexpensive sparkling wine
vermouth, basic port, most sherry, sweet Muscats

WINES THAT REPAY KEEPING

In very general terms, the more expensive a bottle the more it will repay bottle ageing. One simple clue to how long to keep a bottle is (yet again) the principal grape variety from which it was made. Below are some rough guidelines with an approximate number of years in bottle in brackets (although there is considerable variation between wine regions and different vintage conditions):

Red Wines
Cabernet Sauvignon (4-20)
Merlot (2-10)
Pinot Noir (2-8)
Syrah/Shiraz (4-16)
Grenache/Garnacha (2-10)
Nebbiolo (4-20)
Sangiovese (2-8)
Zinfandel (2-6)
Tempranillo of Spain (2-8)

White wines

Riesling (2-30)

Chardonnay (2-6)

Loire Chenin Blanc (4-30)

Petit Manseng of Jurançon (3-10)

and all botrytised wines (5-25)

Storage conditions, about which I shall write elsewhere, can affect the rate at which wine ages.

OUR SENSE OF TASTE

As far as I'm concerned, the enjoyment of wine has to begin with the glass in your hand. Swotting up wine geography and vintage ratings is an optional extra and comes a long way down the line from working out how every drop of wine can give as much pleasure as possible.

THE NOSE

If I could give just one piece of advice to any newcomer to wine, it would be: *don't forget your sense of smell.*

You have only to think of how dull food, even quite strongly flavoured food, tastes when you have a nose blocked by a head cold to realise what an important role the sense of smell plays in what we call taste. Tasting something involves persuading it to release molecules which stimulate special nerve cells in the mouth or the much more discriminating ones in the nose. In fact we can sense flavour only as an aroma because our flavour-sensitive nerve cells are concentrated in a small, postage stamp-sized area at the top of the nose called the olfactory area, which transmits specific messages to the brain, and the only way of getting molecules up there is as a vapour given off by a liquid.

To experience the flavour of a liquid such as wine to the full, therefore, molecules can be encouraged to escape the wine's surface by swirling the wine around before the taster takes a deliberate sniff. Doing this before each mouthful of wine may feel rather pretentious at first, but makes simple good sense. Since man and nature went to so much trouble to put the aromas there, it really does make sense to smell a wine every time you taste it.

THE MOUTH

At this point many wine drinkers may be puzzled. They will reckon they already have a pretty good grasp of wine flavours, without ever having consciously sniffed (or 'nosed', as professional wine tasting parlance has it) a glass in their lives. This is partly because wine naturally vaporises quite easily, and some wines such as those made from Sauvignon Blanc and Riesling grapes are inherently quite aromatic so their molecules need little encouragement to float up the nose. It is also, however, because of the retro-nasal passage which allows some flavour molecules to reach the olfactory area directly from the back of the mouth, without any conscious effort.

This is how most foods are 'tasted'. Food is chewed in the mouth, transforming it into a liquid from which flavour molecules escape up the retro-nasal passage to reach the olfactory area – although many food professionals take just as much trouble consciously to smell ingredients and dishes before consuming them as wine tasters do.

But what of those nerve cells in the mouth? These also have an important, but quite different role to play in the business of tasting, and are what we call taste buds, about 10,000 of them distributed all over the tongue and, to a much lesser extent, the inside of the mouth with a few at the back of the throat. Rather than distinguishing between thousands of different flavours the way the olfactory nerve cells can, taste buds are sensitive to nothing more sophisticated than the basic 'tastes': sourness or acidity, sweetness, bitterness and saltiness (although very few wines taste salty). We all vary enormously in the distribution and concentration of our taste buds.

Wine contains three more components that can have an effect on the inside of the mouth. **Tannin** is a red wine preservative, and has the same tanning effect (as in leather) on the inside of the cheeks as it does when encountered in well-stewed tea. Some tannins can also taste bitter. **Alcohol** has its own, often delightful, effect on our nervous system, but wines that are particularly high in alcohol can leave a 'hot' sensation on the palate after they have been swallowed. And many wines contain a perceptible amount of **fizz**, gassy carbon dioxide, which has a physical, tactile effect which can vary from a gentle prickle to an uncomfortably overwhelming froth. Sometimes winemakers deliberately leave a little carbon dioxide in a wine to make it taste fresher.

HUMAN VARIATION

Almost anyone can be a wine taster: all it takes is a will and a nose. We vary from person to person, not just in terms of the compounds we're particularly sensitive to, and the strength of those sensitivities, but also in our physical make-up. A small minority, sometimes called anosmics, have a poor, defective or damaged sense of smell — either from birth, or the result of polyps, hormonal upsets, head injury, radiation therapy or, most commonly, advancing years.

However, we all have very different sensitivities (and preferences — quite different from what we happen to be able to taste easily) so it's very unlikely that two tasters experience exactly the same sensations when they smell a wine. This is why there are no absolutes in wine tasting. No-one can accuse you of being wrong in your opinion of a wine.

CHOOSING THE RIGHT BOTTLE

How, faced with the array of bottles in a wine store, do you pick the right one off the shelf? Here are a few random but specific suggestions:

- **Decide on a price bracket and stick to it**, but it can be worth spending at the top of that bracket. Remember that in Britain where excise duty alone is about £1.30, the price of the wine inside a bottle selling at £2.99 is about 60p, whereas there is about £1.50 worth of wine in a bottle selling at £4.99 and more than £4 worth in a bottle priced at £9.99. However, a wine that sells for £100 per bottle cannot be said to have £40 worth of wine in the bottle. The additional price may be partly due to the increased cost of land for better vineyards, and perhaps a greater proportion of new oak barrels, but most of the price difference is made up of scarcity, ego or ambition.

- **Take a look at special offers.** In today's competitive marketplace, heavily scrutinised by a bevy of wine critics, these bargains are almost certainly there to lure you into the shop, or make you aware of a new wine rather than to offload rubbish. At least 50 percent of wine sold in the UK is sold on special offer and the increases in sales during the time of a promotion are staggering. Wine producers queue to get a slot in the promotional calendar. But often the 'special offer' price is much closer to the true value of the wine than its supposedly 'regular' price from which it has been discounted. And, unfortunately, few of the most interesting wines feature in these promotions.

- If possible, **pick a bottle that has been on its side**, and has not obviously been kept anywhere the temperature may have varied considerably. Avoid bottles which have been standing upright in strong light (although supermarkets turn their stock over so fast this is not usually a problem and better specialist stores have a policy of constantly changing the one representative bottle from a horizontal lot that is stood upright). Be wary of bottles which have 'wept' around the cork or have a relatively low fill level, as both of these are signs of temperature variation.

- Try to grasp the names at least and ideally the characteristics of the major grape varieties: **Chardonnay, Sauvignon Blanc** and **Riesling** among whites and **Cabernet Sauvignon, Merlot, Pinot Noir** and **Syrah/Shiraz** among reds. If, once you become relatively familiar with the most common wine names, you spot a bottle that seems to have a completely unrecognisable pedigree, give it a try. It is probably there only because someone passionately believes in its inherent quality; wine buyers generally err on the side of caution.

- Be wary of wines designed for early consumption that are more than two years old.

- Remember that very expensive wines carrying vintage dates less than three or four years old are almost certainly years from being fun to drink.

- Try to take a note of any wine you particularly like so that you can find similar styles of wine.

ENTERTAINING WITH WINE

QUANTITIES

A tricky one, this. Individuals' capacity for alcohol varies enormously, as you have doubtless observed yourself. No-one could possibly accuse a host who provided his or her guests with the equivalent of a bottle of wine a head over the course of an evening of meanness. And yet there are some occasions, a weekday lunch for example, at which it would be extremely sophisticated to provide one stunning bottle (of champagne or white burgundy perhaps) for six people, allowing them each one generous glassful of luxury but minimising the dangerous snooze factor of a bibulous lunch.

As a general rule, an average of between half and a bottle a head consumed over several hours at a table makes for a very jolly occasion. If there are many drivers in the party then total consumption should be much less.

Wine served without a meal is potentially much more potent, especially before lunch when most bodies contain little food to buffer alcohol's effect. A quarter of a bottle a head, or two small glasses, could well be enough if there is a significant proportion of abstainers in the group. However, for a long daytime reception, such as a wedding, it would be safer to allow half a bottle a head (and as much as a bottle for an all-evening event). If you're placing a large order most suppliers will allow sale or return.

LIQUIDS AND SOLIDS WITHOUT ALCOHOL

Like many hosts, I frequently overlook the non-alcoholic drinks in my concern to serve just the right wine(s). Try to serve as much water as wine at the table, and to provide a reasonably sophisticated non-alcoholic alternative at parties, such as fizzy mineral water with fresh orange juice or a drop of elderflower syrup, or spiced tomato juice cocktails before lunch. The most delicious non-alcoholic drink I can remember being served was at a book launch hosted by Arabella Boxer. She had prepared a concoction which included cucumber and strawberries, for which the recipe is in her English food book, that was really refreshing, aromatic and non-cloying.

It makes sense not to drink on an empty stomach. Serving something to eat cuts down quite dramatically on the intoxication rate of an alcoholic aperitif. Eating olives out of doors (the only time I encourage my children to throw stones) can seem just right, but they are distractingly Mediterranean and a bit too strongly flavoured for a northern wine like champagne. Radishes, celery, pistachio nuts and quail's eggs are less intrusive, but most of these involve some potentially inconvenient detritus (although halves of quail's egg on a dollop of mayonnaise on toasted rounds of French bread are easy to eat and look glamorous). Little cheesy biscuits, such as the Dutch Roka brand or Fudges' cheese straws, complement most wines, as do Italian breadsticks or *grissini*, even with *prosciutto* wound round them. I also love salted, sautéed almonds, although they can leave fingers pretty greasy.

We have looked at how much wine, water, and non-alcoholic drinks to provide. Here are some specific suggestions as to what sort of wine to serve at which sort of gathering.

PRE-MEAL DRINKS PARTY

Wine (plus a non-alcoholic alternative) is much easier to serve than lots of different mixed drinks. People with carpets tend to prefer to serve white wine, and it is true that many, possibly most, reds are too full-bodied and tannic to be at their best without food. Sparkling wine seems special, but can go to the head very quickly, which may be a problem, or not. A good champagne can be the greatest treat of all, but perfectly well-made, more economical alternatives can be found from Saumur, Limoux, Alsace, California, New Mexico, Australia, New Zealand and England (a cool, or cooled, climate is vital). Still white wines that fit the bill of being light enough but not too acid to drink without food include many not-too-expensive examples from Alsace; dry,

Kabinett and Spätlese wines from Germany (Mosel especially); light Chardonnay and Sauvignon Blanc, Chablis and unoaked examples from the southern hemisphere; well made Pinot Blanc/Bianco and Pinot Gris/Grigio which combine the softness of Pinot with an appetising tang and fresh, lively Verdejo and Albariño from Spain.

ALL-EVENING INFORMAL PARTY

The wines listed above could certainly be served all evening, but after a while your guests may start to crave something more substantial. Red wines that can happily be sipped at with no substantial food to break their fall on the palate tend to be light bodied and low in tannin, such as Beaujolais and other Gamays; red Loire and other Cabernet Franc wines; simpler Merlots; young Pinot Noir (except for most red burgundy);the new generation of juicy young reds from Spain and Portugal; Dolcetto; and, of course, practically any rosé can fit the bill here, particularly those from Spain, which have a fuller, drier taste, nearer to red than white. And if you really are fonder of your carpets than of humouring your guests, you could always switch to a fuller bodied, oaked white such as a Chardonnay or Semillon when you start to serve the food.

EXTENDED LUNCH PARTY

A similar range of wines as for an evening party could be served here, but in smaller quantities perhaps. Warmer weather may require the addition of some examples from the following section.

WINE TO WATCH FOOTBALL (OR OTHER GAMES) WITH

Well, if it's Man U, it has to be red, it seems. Fairly bold so as to provide some anaesthetic against defeat, and slightly syrupy to lubricate the throat. Australian Shiraz fits the bill perfectly.

OUTDOOR WINES

It is usually a waste to serve too fine a wine out of doors, especially in hot weather when the bouquet is lost all too easily to the sun and breeze. Barbecued food, however, calls for its own brand of earthy, robust flavours and, perhaps not too surprisingly, hot climate wines come into their own here, including wines from Australia, the southern Rhône, dry rosés and reds from Provence, practically anything produced on the shores of the Mediterranean, Argentine Malbec, or California Zinfandel.

BEFORE A MEAL

Any of the wines suggested for a pre-meal drinks party make fine aperitifs, as drinks designed to stimulate the appetite are called. The classic aperitif is dry sherry, perhaps too strong and too misunderstood to serve to the uninitiated, but it is one of the wine world's great, undervalued treasures. In warm weather, a freshly opened, chilled bottle of Fino or Manzanilla can give even more concentrated pleasure than a fine white wine (and is the perfect foil for green olives, sweet and juicy *jamon Serrano* and salted almonds) while a dry nutty Amontillado is the perfect antidote to cold weather and an incipient cold. Sercial Madeira can also be beguilingly tingly and a real wake-up call in a glass.

DINNER PARTY

I usually serve an aperitif (see above), one or two (related) first course wines, usually two and sometimes even three different main course wines (moving from lighter to fuller bodied and from young to old), one of which may continue with the cheese but more often (especially since my recent wine and cheese experiments), we move onto a sweet white wine, or strong and sweet wine such as port at the end. But then I want to show off, and this is wildly in excess of what is necessary or even sensible, which is probably an aperitif, a white wine and a red (to cater for those who just can't handle one or other colour). All I would say in my defence is that you learn so much more when comparing similar wines than when drinking them in isolation.

JANCIS ROBINSON

237

AFTER A MEAL

To my mind and palate, sweet wines taste much more delicious drunk on their own (or with cheese) than they do with most sweet food. Any reasonably sweet wine can be delicious after a meal, and those with a fair degree of acidity such as Germans, Austrians, Loire or Jurançon can refresh as well. This is also the time to serve sweet fortified wines (port, sherry, Madeira, marsala, Malaga, liqueur Muscat, southern French and indeed all rich Muscats et al) as well as wine in its strongest, i.e., distilled form: cognac, armagnac and other brandies. The spirit that finds most favour with wine fanatics other than brandy is Chartreuse which, like wine but unlike any other spirit, has an uncanny way of developing in the bottle.

DAYTIME DRINKING

I may be a killjoy, but low alcohol wine seems the crucial element in a bottle to be sprung open for sipping between meals. My good friend the Mosel comes into its own here, as does Italy's panoply of lightly fizzing Moscato, the wrongly reviled Asti included. Buying an example other than the cheapest is the key to enjoyable grapey froth instead of a headache.

FIRST CHOOSE YOUR GLASS

Wine is drunk out of glasses rather than teacups or silver goblets because glass is inert, relatively thin and allows full appreciation of a wine's appearance. The perfect wine glass has a stem and a bowl that goes in towards the rim, so that the aroma is caught within the glass for easy sniffing. It is also made of clear glass so that wine's colour, an important element in assessing and enjoying wine to the full, can be appreciated.

Wine nuts also like to commune with their wine as physically closely as possible, which means that thin crystal is highly valued whereas thicker, patterned and cut glass are not.

So that wine can be swirled without losing any liquid and so that there is space for the precious aroma or bouquet to collect in the bowl, the wine should ideally fill no more than half the available volume of the glass. Not filling up a glass is sensible, not mean.

A stem means that you can hold and swirl the glass without affecting the temperature of the wine with your own body temperature.

There is no real need for a range of glasses of different sizes except that we tend to need smaller servings of sweet wines and fortified wines. It has always seemed unfair to me that white wines are conventionally served in smaller glasses than red wines because they need just as much head space.

Tumblers may be used in earthy and aspiringly earthy Italian restaurants, but the thickness of the glass and the difficulty in swirling the wine around in them makes them pleasure-killers for wine enthusiasts.

The almost spherical **'Paris Goblet'** is one of the cheapest wine glasses available (four can be bought for the price of a very basic wine). It fulfils the criteria of having a stem and going in towards the rim, and is better than narrower 'tulip' shapes, but the glass is too thick to provide intimate or luxurious contact with the wine.

The **ISO tasting glass**, like a large tulip on a short stem, was designed in the 1970's by the International Standards Organisation advised by a panel of professional wine tasters including Michael Broadbent MW. For a long time is was regarded as the standard professional wine glass. Machine-made versions are available and cost no more than the cheapest bottle of wine. Hunt around on the internet as they're rarely available in wine shops, except around Christmas. It does the job but certainly wins no prizes for glamour and more and more professionals find it just too small and clunky.

Riedel, a family company based in the Austrian Tyrol, is by far the most successful and admired producer of glassware specifically designed for wine drinkers. Working on the principle that how the liquid hits the tongue affects how it will taste, the Riedel family of Austria have developed slightly different glass designs for wine types. These include, for example, young and mature red Bordeaux, non-vintage and vintage champagne, vintage port and tawny port, Chianti Classico and Brunello di Montalcino etc. All of this is a bit much for most homes (including mine) but there are much more affordable, machine-made versions available which provide much more pleasure than the standard ISO glass – and infinitely more than a Paris goblet. They recently launched and successfully created a fashion for a range of stemless glasses.

Riedel have now bought Spiegelau, once their main rival, although Schott is independent of them. Now that wine is such a growth area, all manner of outfits such as Waterford are becoming interested in expensive crystal specially designed for wine. Cristal d'Arques dominates the French glass business with Baccarat at the top end.

The only non-standard glass shape you might think of investing in is a tall, thin glass for sparkling wines (often called a flute), which allows minimal escape of the carbon dioxide dissolved in the wine which makes it sparkle, lets you see a long journey for each bubble, and is a suitably glamorous shape in itself. The old-fashioned coupe, supposedly modelled on Marie-Antionette's breast, is very easy to spill and encourages the precious carbon dioxide to escape as fast as possible. Riedel make a very versatile and inexpensive tulip-shaped champagne glass.

Specialist retailers of wine glasses in the UK include Around Wine in London W1 and *www.wineware.co.uk*.

DECANTERS, DECANTING AND CARING FOR GLASSWARE

DECANTERS

You can use any clean, watertight vessel to decant (pour the contents of) a bottle into. A china jug would do but glass is provably inert and has the great advantage of allowing you to enjoy looking at the colour of the wine (especially attractive for white wines). Proper, traditional decanters tend to be glass with a narrow neck so you can pour them easily and with a stopper so you can decide whether or not to keep air out.

Decanters tend to come in single or double-bottle (magnum) sizes. Antique ones can be unearthed from junk shops for relatively little money, especially since you don't strictly need a stopper for a decanter used only for serving.

Madeira can be kept in a (stoppered) decanter virtually forever, but port and even sherry tend to deteriorate after a week or sometimes less. Wine that has not been strengthened by alcohol is often worse (and occasionally, in the case of concentrated, tannic monsters, better) after 24 hours in a decanter.

TO DECANT OR NOT

There are strong practical reasons for separating a wine with sediment from that sediment which can taste bitter and physically gets in the way of enjoyment. This traditionally involves standing the bottle upright for a few hours beforehand – the time needed varies with the amount and quality of sediment – and pouring the wine into another clean glass container with a strong light source behind the bottleneck so that you can tell when the sediment is about to slip into the neck and can stop pouring at that point. That light source could be a candle or any strong light such as a desk light, table lamp without the shade or strip lighting under a wall-mounted cupboard. Bear in mind that some wines coat the inside of the bottle with a deposit that will not fall to the bottom of the bottle however long you stand it upright – but nor will it make the wine cloudy.

I often decant full boded white wines which may have no sediment at all, simply because they look so gorgeously golden in a decanter. A glass jug or clean bottle would do just as well in practical terms. In the famous Locanda Cipriani on Torcello in the Venice lagoon, local fizzy white Prosecco is served in vast glass jugs.

Scientists say we should decant at the last possible moment so that no part of the wine's reaction with air be lost to us. As a host, I confess I am prepared to sacrifice completeness for expediency with all but the most fragile old wines, say those over 25 years old, depending on their body and the style of the vintage. In practice, therefore, I tend to decant most wines that need decanting just before guests arrive, saving only really old bottles to be decanted just before serving.

Some young wines, however, are so tight and closed that, even though they are too young to have formed any sediment, they benefit from the aeration involved in pouring the wine from a closed bottle into another container. If I'm decanting for this reason, I'll deliberately splash the wine as much as possible in a glass container with quite a wide neck.

I also find a stainless steel funnel with a fine mesh, or a clean funnel with coffee filter paper useful for rescuing the wine from bottles into which corks have crumbled.

Here are some very rough practical guidelines for serious, reasonably expensive examples of the wine types cited below:

Decant immediately before serving:
Red Bordeaux and Rhône more than 20 years old
Vintage port more than 50 years old

Decant 1–2 hours before serving:
Red Bordeaux and Rhône five to 20 years old

Vintage port 10–50 years old

Decant splashily for maximum aeration up to 4 hours before serving:
Red Bordeaux and Rhône less than five years old
Barolo, Barbaresco and Brunello
Modern Rioja, Ribera del Duero and Priorat
Bairrada, Dão and Douro reds
Vintage port less than 10 years old
Ambitious New World Cabernet and Syrah/Shiraz

CARING FOR GLASSWARE

Aesthetically, glassware needs to be clean and has the annoying habit of being extremely breakable and showing every speck or dribble. The important thing as far as wine is concerned is that the glass smells of nothing – not washing up liquid (which can stop the formation of bubbles in fizzy wine), and certainly not dirty glass cloths. Many smart wine glasses, including much of the Riedel range, are perfectly happy in a domestic dishwasher and indeed benefit from the high temperatures there. Water has to be soft, however, and there is no need for detergent. Hand washing glasses achieves best results if glasses are washed in very hot water, rinsed in cold, and polished immediately with linen tea towels reserved for the purpose – I'm told. In an ideal world, we would all have unlimited supplies of new, fine, crystal glasses.

Decanters are notoriously difficult to clean inside. Standing them full of a warm solution of denture cleanser can work. I'm also told that a product called Magic Balls, which come in small pots, cost very little, and are available from good kitchenware shops, do the job well too, although I have not first hand experience. They come with a small sieve ready to pour the balls into, rinse through and dry on kitchen paper before putting back into their little pot. These also work for wine glasses, apparently, if you have hard water and they've turned milky in the dishwasher.

MATCHING WINE AND FOOD

With its relatively low alcoholic strength, appetizing acidity and lack of sickly artificial flavours, wine is the perfect accompaniment to food. Am I kidding myself that a well chosen wine makes food taste better? Surely not . . .

The most important rule about food and wine matching is that there are no rules. You can drink any wine at all with any food — even red wine with fish! — and the world will continue to revolve. Anyone who thinks worse of you for serving the 'wrong' wine is stuffy, prejudiced and probably ill-informed. There are, however, some very simple guidelines for getting the most out of particular foods and bottles.

1. The single most important aspect of a wine for food matching is not colour but body or weight (which corresponds closely with alcoholic strength).

2. The second most important aspect are tannins for reds and sweetness for whites.

3. Try to match a wine's body to the power of the strongest ingredient in the food. Serve delicate flavoured foods such as simple white fish or poached chicken with lighter bodied wines and stronger, more robust foods such as grilled tuna with spiced lentils or osso buco with full bodied wines. Many white wines will do jobs which are conventionally regarded as red wine jobs, and vice versa.

4. A tannic wine such as one made from Cabernet Sauvignon, Nebbiolo and most Portuguese reds, can taste softer when served with chewy foods, notably unsauced red meat (sauces are almost invariably more powerful than what they are saucing and are usually a better guide to the ideal wine accompaniment).

5. All wines taste horribly acid if served with sweet food, unless

they are sweeter than the foot itself – which seriously limits the choice to be served with most sweet courses to wines such as Vouvray moelleux, Alsace SGN, Sauternes, German Trockenbeerenauslese and Beerenauselese and some sweet sherries. It also makes wine purists wary of sweet relishes. (But sweetish wines can go surprisingly well with savoury food – a Vouvray demi-sec can taste gorgeous with a savoury creamy sauce, for example – while sweet wines can go well with cheeses on the sweet and salt principle, as in melon and prosciutto). Very acid foods such as citrus fruits and vinegar can do funny things to seriously fine, perfectly balanced wine, but can flatter a slightly acid wine (from a particularly cool climate or year) by making it taste less sour. Similarly, freshly ground black pepper might distort our impression of a complex, venerable wine but acts as a sensitising agent on most palates and flatters young, light wines by making them taste fuller and richer.

DIFFICULT FOODS FOR WINE

There are very few foods that destroy wine, but very hot spices tend to stun the taste buds so that you could still smell a wine but would find it impossible to experience its dimensions because the palate's sensory equipment is ablaze. Globe artichokes and, to a lesser extent, asparagus tend to make wine taste oddly metallic, and dense chocolate is so sweet and mouth-coating that it too can be difficult (but not impossible) to match with wine. A far greater enemy to wine than any food, however, is toothpaste. Also, don't forget how wine styles can be manipulated by care with serving temperatures.

The increasing importance of vegetables and salads has had its own sunny influence on food and wine matching. Their direct flavours can seem better suited for New World wines that the dusty complexity of many an Old World classic.

COOKING WITH WINE

There is a school of thought that any wine used in cooking should be top quality and/or of the same region as the dish. As a mean Northerner, I find this hard to accept, particularly as so little research has been done on exactly what happens to wine when you cook with it. I am sure that if the wine in the dish (as in steeped strawberries, for example) is never heated, then it is worth choosing one that tastes as delicious as you can afford. If you want to reduce a sauce using wine, however, I would have thought you wanted one with as much body as possible — and that the wine's components may go through so many transformations that the initial flavour could not possibly be preserved. More research, please! Meanwhile, in our household we will continue to see cooking as a particularly satisfying way of using up wine leftovers.